Eat Your Vegetables, Bitches!

Plant-Based Recipes for Foodies

Over 140 Recipes to Tantalize Your Tastebuds

~ *Lisa Flowers* ~

Photography by Eric Green

IngramSpark
La Vergne, Tennessee

Eat Your Vegetables, Bitches

First Edition, 2021
Digital Edition, 2021

Published and Distributed by:

Ingram Book Grouyp, LLC
One Ingram Boulevard
La Vergne, Tennessee 3708
615.793.5000
www.ingramspark.com

ISBN: 978-0-9968579-1-8

Cover and Book Graphic Design and Layout: Andrew Alfe

Dedication

To my family and friends who always support and cheer me on,
and all who chance to open these pages,
I dedicate this collection of recipes to feed your souls!
May you be a brave cook and may you be well and happy!
Bon appetit!

TO: Saida & Alan H

Be well, Happy and
Bold in the Kitchen!
You are Awesome!

Lisa Powers

Acknowledgments

Victoire (Vicky) Henderson, my steadfast food buddy, sous chef and confidant. You are always ready to taste! Thank you for all the help you have so kindly and generously given.
I don't know what I would have done without you!

Kim Bogan Goldman, my best friend in the world. Thank you for the whimsical title for this book that you threw out to me in jest. I bet you never thought I would say, "That is IT!" It is so Us! I am grateful for all the years of fun and food we have spent together. May we never stop cooking! And eating!

Paul Williams – Sincere thanks to you for being my food taster, even when you thought something was weird. I appreciate you always supporting me in all my endeavors and giving me the message that you want to, "Water me and watch me grow." What a gift!

Tom Barillier - Your support and encouragement during this Time of COVID has meant more to me than you know. I look forward to the day when you can actually taste my food, as opposed to a Messenger blow by blow!

Eric Green - Photographer. I so appreciate your hard work and dedication to this project. Your photographs are beautiful! You give new meaning to the phrase, "Will work for food."
Thank you!

Andrew Alfe - You have taken my work and turned it into a beautiful book! Thank you for your patience and kindness through this process.

Chef Lisa Flowers and Photographer Eric Green

Eat Your Vegetables, Bitches

Table of Contents

Green Things, Yellow Things, Red Things, Orange Things AKA: Vegetables   59

Main Courses   75

On the Side

Bean, Beans!

Sauces and Such...

Salads and Whatnot 173

Salad Dressings 197

Soups and Stews 205

Sweets for the Sweet

Themed Menu Plans

Index

Introduction

Introduction

It has been a long road, but I am here at last, writing the companion cookbook to 'Real Food: The Ultimate Medicine ~ Happiness: The Natural Side Effect.' When I wrote the book I was dipping my toe in and out of the vegetarian and vegan world. I don't know about you, but becoming a Plant-Based eater was a long process for me. Years, in fact! I have done a lot of back and forth dancing with this important life change, and I now understand why it can be so difficult to walk away from these rich, salty, meaty and cheesy foods that are so available in our culture. And, it took a physical wake up call to move me steadfastly into a (mainly) Whole Foods Plant-Based way of living and thriving!

I had been plagued with migraine headaches since my early 20's. I had no idea what these headaches were when they started. Honestly, most of the time I assumed it was a hangover. As I got a little older, and became a sober person (28 years! Thank you very much!) I knew it had to be something else. I did not see auras nor was I banished to a dark room for hours or days on end. By that time I had three children and I had things to do!   I discovered that Imitrex would get rid of the migraines. That was the good news! The bad news was the residual fogginess, feeling cranky, my skin was sensitive to hot water, my excellent memory was…shall we say not at all what it once was, and I experienced a general feeling of being drugged. It was not fun.

I tried everything to conquer the migraines. Food allergy testing, food elimination diets, acupuncture, craniosacral therapy, chiropractic, homeopathy, naturopathic doctors, hormonal therapy, counseling, hypnotherapy, vitamin supplements, all kinds of weird and wonderful supplements, allopathic doctors, preventive medications, and so on, ad nauseum. Don't get me wrong, a lot of these treatments were beneficial in some ways and led me to the next indicated step, but I was still having many migraines each month, sometimes fifteen or more. And what was just as painful were the medication side effects that I had been experiencing for about 20 years of taking Imitrex. With everything I tried, I truly thought my choices were migraine headaches or medication with all the wretched side effects. Although, there was this voice inside me that periodically whispered, "You need to go away somewhere and totally detox. Be in a place where you can rest and have a headache for as many days as necessary in order to get EVERYTHING out of your system." I knew that voice was right. But of course I was the mother of three children and they came first for me. And, I had no idea where I would go to detox, even if I could manage to get away.

As a Holistic Health Coach and Clinical Hypnotherapist it really pissed me off that I could help people with health and emotional issues, but I seemingly could not help myself with this horrible cloud of endless migraine headaches.

It was not until I discovered True North Health Center that I became free of migraines, and, have been ever since! I heard about True North when my dear friend, Lynn, was diagnosed with cancer. After surgery she chose to forgo chemotherapy and radiation and packed her bags and headed to Santa Rosa, California, and True North Health Center. True North offers a unique form of treatment for myriad health issues. Medically Supervised Water Only Fasting! Yup, that's right…Water Only!

Humans and animals have been water fasting since the beginning of time. Notice what a dog or a cat will do when they are under the weather; they will lie down and sleep and only drink water. Smart humans do this, too!

It took two years for me to say Yes to True North after Lynn went and came back looking 20 years younger, lean, healthy and feeling good. I am a processor and I do not make decisions quickly. Ask anyone who knows me. But when I finally did start to research True North, it became more and more clear that this was my next indicated step. After all, I had tried everything else! I filled out and submitted the health history form online. Three days later I got a call from the founder of True North Health Center, Dr. Alan Goldhamer. Little did I know that this was protocol for him. He calls everyone who takes the time to fill out the medical history and is considering True North as a treatment option. *At this point, I believe there is a fee for this initial call with Dr. Goldhamer. To me Dr. Goldhamer is a bit of a celeb, having seen him in various documentaries. And I have great respect for him as an expert in the field of wellness. So, I tucked away my fandom and had a life-changing conversation with the good doctor. By the time the call ended, I was booked to stay at True North and to experience Medically Supervised Water Only Fasting.

True North is a popular medical facility, so I was booked three and a half months out. Dr. Goldhamer was very specific about what I might want to do to prepare my body for my stay. He recognized that I was way ahead of the game health wise because of my profession as a Holistic Health Coach, meaning I was not on the S.A.D. or Standard American Diet. But, fasting is fasting and detoxing is some real shit! No pun intended. So, he told me I might want to adopt a fully whole foods plant based diet leading up to my stay and, eat only vegetables and fruit for three or four days before my arrival if I wanted to lessen my suffering. Hell yes, I wanted to lessen my suffering! I heard that suggestion loud and clear! I am a wimp when it comes to suffering, so I took his advice and am grateful I did!

I arrived on Friday January 18th, 2019. I had a migraine that day and had taken Imitrex. I was a little nervous because I am not a great faster.

I met my amazing doctor the next morning, Dr. Csilla Veress (pronounced Chilla Veresh…coolest name ever!) and she started me on Water Only Fasting that morning. She asked me how long I thought I needed to fast. I said 7-10 days. She said for migraines I needed 14 days of Water Only. So, that is what I did. I consumed nothing but pure distilled water for 14 days. On day 15 I was given green juice. Day 16 I ate steamed zucchini. Day 17 was salad. And when I say salad, I mean a huge variety of greens, shredded zucchini, carrots, fennel, beets, onions, tomatoes, broccoli, peppers…you know: Vegetables! Day 18 I added whole grains and Beans! Days 19 and 20 I ate everything they had, all completely whole foods and plant based. Oh, and did I mention it was SOS free? That is, no Salt, Oil or Sugar. Pretty intense, but with pure and clean taste buds everything tasted so good! And speaking of taste buds…

Anyone who eats the S.A.D. (Standard American Diet) will have taste buds that are hyper stimulated every day. Consequently, when someone eats real food that is simple and natural, they might think it is tasteless. But it does not take long to retrain the taste buds. It's pretty simple; eat Real Food that is not gussied up with tons of salt, oil, sugar, or anything artificial. Your taste buds will relax and begin to enjoy the taste of Food au Natural!

Eat Your Vegetables, Bitches

Before I arrived at True North, I was pretty darned healthy! At least I thought I was. I ate lots of vegetables and fruit, I did not eat a lot of sugary treats. I ate beans, nuts and seeds, truly whole grains and I was gluten free because I cannot tolerate gluten. It makes me foggy and cranky. In other words, I was doing a lot of things right food-wise. What I did not understand was that I was caught in what Dr. Doug Lisle and Dr. Alan Goldhamer called, 'The Pleasure Trap'. This is the title of their book, which I highly recommend to anyone who finds themselves dieting, binging, overeating, and craving sugary, salty, meaty, fatty foods…AKA: The Standard American Diet. These two brilliant doctors go to great lengths to explain why we crave the salt, fat and sugar that takes the lead in North American cuisine.

You see, we are biologically programmed to gravitate toward the highest calorie, highest fat containing foods because our ancestors either did or died. Literally. But, hold the phone…that was when food was scarce and there was a real danger of starving to death. On the North American continent, and many other places on Earth today food is not scarce and the high calorie, over salted, high fat foods that many people consume on a daily basis are the #1 reason for the chronic diseases that are killing good people every day, and also putting our children at risk of dying sooner than their parents.

The Big Food industry, including the Dairy, Beef, Pork, Chicken and Egg Agri-businesses, have gone to the ends of the Earth to brainwash the good citizens of the world into thinking that their products are healthful. There is too much published research out today about the health and environmental ramifications of a meat, dairy, egg-based diet. It is just not sustainable, for us or for the planet.

I came away from True North with the knowledge that I over salted my food, I found it hard to say no thank you to an ice cream cone once in a while or desert when it was around, or cheese at a potluck, etc. As healthy as I am, my taste buds were still hijacked.

Then we have the people in our lives who question how we will possibly be able to survive without eating animal products. The real question should be; how are we surviving now? And more importantly, are we thriving? In most cases those answers would be, not well, and no. Let's explore one of the most common concerns of people who do not yet understand the science behind a plant based way of living.

But, Where Will You Get Your Protein?

Eat Your Vegetables, Bitches

Ahhh…where have I heard this question before? If you are vegetarian or vegan, I know you have been asked about how you will possibly get enough protein. So many people are hyper focused on protein. Yes, protein is an important nutrient that we need in order to repair, restore and maintain the tissues in our body. Muscles, bones, organs, blood, skin, hair and nails all rely on protein to be healthy.

Science lesson: Protein is a nutrient that is made up of 21 amino acids. Our bodies can naturally make 12 of these amino acids, but for the remaining 9 we must rely on the foods we eat.

Now, as for the idea that we humans need excessive amounts of protein, well, the response would be Poppycock! Think about the strongest mammals on the planet: gorillas, rhinos, elephants. These magnificent beasts are all vegetarians. So, the idea that we need protein from animal foods in order to be strong and healthy gets tossed out with the salami. High protein diets can be dangerous in several ways. First, these high protein diets (you know what I am talking about) are mostly animal protein based, and with animal protein you also get saturated fats, excess calories and virtually no micronutrients. When I say micronutrients, I mean the real nutrition our bodies need in order to thrive.

All food contains protein. Vegetables, fruits, nuts, seeds, beans, grains…I will say that again:

ALL FOODS HAVE PROTEIN!

Another problem with excessive protein is that the body does not store protein. It is either converted to fat or excreted through the kidneys, contributing to kidney stones and osteoporosis. Also, there was a meta-analysis of 31 studies on disease and the intake of protein published by the *International Scholarly Research Network* which concluded that, "Overconsumption of protein was associated with higher rates of cancer, osteoporosis, renal disease, disorders of liver function and coronary artery disease." Source: *Real Food Network*

Check out Valter Longo, PhD and his 2014 study in Cell Metabolism.

Dr. Valter Longo and his team are comparing a high protein diet, particularly proteins from animals, to be almost as bad for your health as smoking cigarettes. But, all proteins are not created equal! According to Dr. Longo's study's conclusions, "The negative health associations of a high protein intake were reduced or eliminated if the proteins came from plants."

So, where will WE get our protein? That's right! Vegetables, fruits, nuts, seeds, beans and whole grains. Yes, ALL foods have protein, and if one eats a well-balanced Whole Foods Plant Based diet you will get enough protein. And, you will greatly reduce the risks of Cancer, Heart Disease, Diabetes, High Blood Pressure, High Cholesterol, Alzheimer's Disease, and other diseases. And, you will gain nutrition, vitamins, minerals, amino acids, healthy fats, carbohydrates and protein that your body so craves!

Children and Sugar

Have you ever seen a child after a birthday party, when the cake and ice cream have settled in and the sugar high has started to wear off? Or when the artificial colors from the icing on that birthday cake makes a child start screaming?   Well, breakfast cereal is not far behind birthday cake, in some instances. So many of us these days have sensitivities to foods. And one of the biggest offenders is Sugar! And, not just sugar, but all the additives, preservatives, artificial colors and flavors, and/or saturated fats that usually accompany sugar laden foods, and I am using the word 'foods' very loosely. I hate to tell you this, because I know how we all love our sweets, but sugar is addictive. Period. The more we eat, the more we want. You may not want to eat large quantities of sugar, but in most cases people feed their sugar addiction on a daily basis, sometimes without even knowing it. Often times, all day long. There is sugar in almost EVERYTHING! You can rarely buy packaged, processed foods without Sugar being a headliner or at least an extra. I am not saying one should never indulge in a sweet treat, but if we were to look at treats as something special and not an everyday occurrence we would all be a lot healthier. Because guess what? The sugar draws you in with its alluring sweetness, but what is most likely waiting for you as well is a load of fat like butter, shortening or oils in that donut, muffin, cake, cookie, ice cream, caramel macchiato. And the saturated fat is what is really a health issue.

Keep in mind when you are reading labels, and I strongly recommend reading labels, that four grams of sugar equals one teaspoon or one cube of sugar. So, you do the math. Better yet, have your children do the math! Let them be part of the process. When your child is having one cup of cereal in the morning that has 15 grams of sugar, that is equal to about four teaspoons or 4 cubes of sugar! Holy Cow! That is a lot of sugar! Then we send them off to school and expect them to sit still and learn! What? Then they go to the lunchroom and are served processed and packaged food-like substances, or they take a Lunchable from home. Children have about fifteen minutes to eat and about fifteen minutes to play at recess, if they are lucky. Then once again, they go back to class and are expected to sit still and learn.

Our kiddos deserve better than this. We are in charge of our children's health and wellbeing. Does it not make sense to ensure that what they put into their precious growing bodies is pure and nutritious? I say YES! It makes perfect sense. As a matter of fact, it is our responsibility to provide healthy, nutritious food for these young people. Children learn by example and by doing, so when we, the adults make healthy choices by cooking fresh Real Food, the children will follow suit. We wouldn't allow our kiddos to not brush their teeth, go without a daily bath, or play with fire or a loaded gun would we? It is all part of the package. We parents need to be in charge!

I have often seen children "reacting" to foods they have eaten. It is so common that society has given these reactions other names like, ADD, ADHD, Oppositional Defiant Disorder, Anxiety Disorder, Mood Disorder, Eating Disorder, etc. I am not saying these "Disorders" are always about foods, but as a Holistic Health Coach and Mother of three, when a child is experiencing difficulties with health and emotions, my first question is, "What is the child eating?" It is a valid question!

How to Kill Yourself on a Budget

Eat Your Vegetables, Bitches

The Standard American Diet is S.A.D. Cheap food…it's everywhere! McDonald's boasts "New! Buy One, Get One For $1 Includes Quarter Pounder and 10 Piece Chicken Nuggets". This kind of irresponsible corporate behavior is one of the reasons poverty and chronic diseases are interconnected. These cheap, fatty, salty, sugary super unhealthy foods are advertised In Your Face everywhere we go. People who don't have a lot of money, time and information are all over the idea of spending a couple of dollars for lunch, dinner, breakfast, snacks, whatever! This is very true of our young people, the people who will grow up and may have babies one day and, perpetuate the chronic disease epidemic that has been created in part by the availability of these cheap and toxic foods. And this type of food is addictive! Our taste buds get hijacked by the salt, fat and sugar, and real food cannot compete, not when folks are accustomed to chemicalized foods that are actually lab tested to create cravings. Not kidding, Folks!

Most people have been on one diet or another in their life. Many people have been on myriad diets! Why is the Diet industry so huge? Why do people spend BILLIONS of dollars each year on weight loss foods, products, pills, diets and surgeries? And the truth is, we are fatter and sicker than ever! Why? Because diets don't work! Diets don't work, and that is the money maker. People keep trying the next new thing on the market. The next promise, the next fad. And I will say it again; The Big Food Industry has HIJACKED your taste buds! Even "diet" foods are overly salty and or sweet. The solution to the health issues that are epidemic in our country is The Food! In order to prevent and reverse Obesity, Diabetes, Heart Disease, High Blood Pressure, Cancer, and/or Alzheimer's Disease, we must first change the foods we are eating. It really is that simple. It's not easy, but it is that simple.

If only the Big Food Industry was not operating as The Upside Down! For those who are not Stranger Things fans, that means that Big Food is not at all what it seems. We see advertising for "Milk…It Does a Body Good", "Beef…It's What's For Dinner", "Pork…The New White Meat". As if these products were actually what we need as a species for health and vitality. What we need to do is turn the food industry on its head and make vegetables and fruits inexpensive! Let's make the slogans, 'Veggies…This is What's For Dinner!' 'Fruit…The Sweetest Treat to Eat!', 'Beans…The New Protein!' It boggles my mind that on the North American continent there is more chronic disease than anywhere in the world, and we have the crappiest diet. And, as other countries adopt the American fast food "restaurants", their chronic disease statistics are going up. Hmmm…could there be a connection? We are the wealthiest country in the world, and the sickest! Okay, let's not dwell on the negative. Let's focus on what we can do to prevent and reverse some of these chronic diseases!

Eat Real Foods, move your body every day, meditate, be grateful, be helpful, be kind, drink purified water, breathe deeply. Honestly, it's really not complicated. The difficult part is people don't usually want to make changes unless they are backed into a corner. That corner is usually Cancer, Heart Disease, Diabetes, Irritable Bowel Syndrome, High Blood Pressure, High Cholesterol, Depression, in other words a health crisis. Why not skip the crisis and make the changes necessary to avoid the crisis? Ponder that, will you?

When you cook at home, you are guaranteed to know what you are eating and are able to really increase the nutritional value of the foods. Eating out is fine once in a while, but restaurants often buy packaged and processed foods and dress them up. The food is over salted, has excessive amounts of oils, fat and sugar, and it is often simply not fresh. So, cook at home whenever possible. Hey, here is a cookbook to assist you!

You Are What You Eat. Period.

Eat Your Vegetables, Bitches

If what you are eating is unhealthy, how does that affect your everyday living? How does what you eat affect how well you think and feel? And, are we happy when we feel like crap because we have eaten crap? My guess would be No. With so many children and adults eating nutritionally bankrupt food-like substances on a daily basis, it is amazing that anyone can function and have Happiness in life.

But I guarantee when you start eating a clean diet of REAL FOOD, you will feel the difference! When you begin to add in real foods, vegetables, fruits, nuts and seeds, beans and whole grains, and crowding out "foods" full of white flour and sugar, processed oils, animal products and artificial everything you will notice the shift in your emotional wellbeing, your state of mind, and your general feelings of Happiness! Your skin will glow, your energy level will skyrocket, you will sleep better, chances are hormones will level out, sex drive will increase and you will feel good! You will be amazed at how powerful food really is; healthy foods and unhealthy foods.

It's really not that complicated. Most people know what they should be doing for their health, but have a hard time implementing changes. Why? Because our taste buds have been commandeered by processed foods with an abundance of salt, oil and sugar! These substances create a vicious cycle of cravings, and unless we eliminate processed food-like substances we will forever be on the merry-go-round of craving junk! And, the fact is, our children are getting sick. Children are being diagnosed with Type 2 Diabetes, previously known as Adult Onset Diabetes. This is the first generation EVER whose parents have a good chance of outliving their children. That is a crime.

In the pages that follow I will lay out simple and delicious recipes for making Real Food for yourself, your family and your friends! And, I know you will feel good and make some important, easily attainable lifestyle changes on your Happiness Quest for True Wellness!

Real Food: The Ultimate Medicine ~ Happiness: The Natural Side Effect!
Let's Journey!
So, why are we here? Oh yes! This is a cookbook, and so…

The Diet

Good God, NO! This book is not another diet book!

News flash: DIETS DON'T WORK! But I guarantee you will not hear that from the media. Why? Because the diet industry is BIG business! Americans alone spend more than $60 BILLION annually, from diet pills to programs to weight loss surgery. People want to lose weight. But I believe there is a shift happening in the diet industry because of the simple fact that people don't just want to lose weight. What people ultimately want is to be healthy. This is good news!

So, when I say diets don't work, what exactly does that mean? If you have ever been on a diet you probably know what I mean. Diets, in most cases equal depravation of some sort; eat this amount of certain foods, but only in combination with these other foods. Or, don't eat this, but eat lots of that. Or, eat this type of food in the morning. Then another diet tells you NEVER eat that food in the morning. Carbs are bad. Carbs are good. Don't drink coffee. Coffee is good for you. Coconut oil and avocado are fattening. Coconut oil and avocado are Super Foods! Soy causes cancer. Soy prevents cancer. Then we have all the packaged, processed, chemical laden "Diet" foods. Also known as cancer in a box. WTH! No wonder we have an obesity epidemic in our country. And, it is serious! People die every day from the diseases and health issues associated with obesity. A person cannot stick to a "diet" indefinitely, and once you come off the diet, what happens? The weight almost invariably creeps back, and then some! You know what I am talking about! Or you know someone who knows what I am talking about.

With the Plant Based recipes in this book you will find ease and joy as you shift into this healthy and kind way of eating. It is not a struggle to make changes in your diet when what you are changing is nasty food anyway. There will be no calorie counting, no carb or protein counting. Just simply eating real food in variety will transform your whole concept of "dieting". Your mind will clear, as well as your skin! The ways in which you think of "dieting" will transform naturally as you learn to eat clean foods that are gentle on the environment!

90/10

There are many people in the world who have no problem switching to a full-on Whole Foods Plant Based way of living and never look back. I am not one of those people. I go out to restaurants, I go to friend's homes for dinner, I go to parties…I live my life fully in the world of food! And I really try not to impose my food choices on my hosts. So, for me that means I eat a WFPB diet 90+% of the time, and I don't sweat the other 10%. Freedom Baby!

The Solution: Eat Real Food

We talked about this in 'Real Food: The Ultimate Medicine ~ Happiness: The Natural Side Effect'. If you have not read it yet, please do! To eat Real food is the solution to a lot of the health issues plaguing North America today, and for the past seventy years. With the introduction of "convenience" foods came the huge increase of heart disease, cancer, diabetes and Alzheimer's. Spam, frozen dinners, McDonald's…Our country went from home cooking to opening packages. And with that comes dis-ease.

Let's talk food! What is real food? Vegetables, fruits, nuts and seeds, legumes, whole grains, all organic (whenever you can) and without added sugar or unnatural ingredients. And so…

Breakfast of Champions!

Eat Your Vegetables, Bitches

Breakfast of Champions!

The most important meal of the day?

Yes, especially when you think of what breakfast is: Breaking Your Fast. But breakfast does not have to be early in the morning right after you get up. And, it certainly does not have to be bacon and eggs! Whatever you eat first thing in your day is Breakfast, so be creative! A Smoothie is a simple and nutritious choice for breakfast. My Smoothie recipes are full of greens and berries, which happen to be two of the most nutrient dense foods on the planet. Or maybe you are a hearty breakfast eater. In that case go for it with a Veggie Tofu Scramble and Rise & Shine Potatoes, or a Breakfast Burrito. Lots of choices…have fun!

Gluten Free Granola

Serves 4

1/2 cup gluten free oats
1/2 cup flax meal
1/4 cup (heaping) raw pumpkin seeds
1 cup raw chopped cashews
1 TBLS vanilla
1/4 cup real maple syrup

1/4 cup olive oil
1 cup whole almonds, I like to use roasted and lightly salted
1/2 cup slivered almonds
1/2 cup chopped walnuts
1/4 cup dried fruit of your choice -
      cranberries, raisins, cherries.

Preheat the oven to 325 degrees.

Combine the oats, flax meal, pumpkin seeds, 1/2 cup of cashews, vanilla, maple syrup and olive oil in a large bowl. Toss to coat everything well. Spray a cookie sheet well with olive oil or canola spray. Spread the mixture onto the cookie sheet into an even layer approximately 1/2 inch of thickness. Bake for 18 minutes or until it is nearly dry and crispy. DO NOT OVERCOOK! KEEP AN EYE ON IT!

Allow the mixture to cool completely in the pan for about 45 minutes. After about 20 minutes loosen the mixture from the pan with a spatula and allow to continue cooling.

While the mixture is baking, combine the two types of almonds, the walnuts, the rest of the cashews and the dried fruit in the same bowl you used before.

Crumble the cooled mixture into the bowl of nuts and dried fruit. Stir well and store in the freezer. Serve with a scoop of vegan yogurt and/or fresh fruit.

Eat Your Vegetables, Bitches

Breakfast Burritos/Tacos

Serves 4

Corn or flour tortillas
1 recipe Tofu Scramble
1 potato, diced
Vegan sausage (optional)

Sriracha
Vegan cheddar cheese (optional)
Fresh Mexican Salsa Olé or your favorite salsa
Salt and pepper

Put the diced potatoes in a pot of water and bring to a boil on high heat. Simmer for about 5 minutes, until soft, not falling apart. Drain and set aside.

In a sauté pan cook the vegan sausage, crumbling as it cooks. Drain fat. Make the recipe for Veggie Tofu Scramble adding a good squirt of Sriracha. Add in the cooked potatoes, vegan sausage and combine well.

Heat the tortillas in the microwave or over the flame on a gas stove. With a flour tortilla lying flat in front of you, fill with Veggie Tofu Scramble mixture, salsa and vegan cheese, off center towards you. Fold the sides in then roll tortilla away from you! If you are using corn tortillas fill them like tacos! Enjoy!

Eat Your Vegetables, Bitches

Veggie Tofu Scramble

Serves 3 - 4

Okay confession…my dear friend, Paul is Tofu-Phobic. He thinks he doesn't like tofu. But he has never really tried it…or so he thought. MuuHaHaHa (insert Evil laughter here!). So, one Sunday morning I made Brunch for us: Scrambled Eggs with Veggies, Rise & Shine Potatoes and Sourdough toast. Every morsel was devoured! Little did he know the "eggs" were actually tofu. He was not amused, but sometimes we have to go around the corner to get down the street! Whatever that means…Enjoy Brunch!

Olive Oil or Canola Spray
1/2 medium onion, diced
1/2 tsp turmeric
1 small zucchini, diced
2 cloves garlic, minced
1 tsp tamari, soy sauce or Bragg's Liquid Aminos
1 – 12 oz container firm or extra firm tofu, drained on paper towels and cut into 1" cubes
1/2 bell pepper, any color diced
1 cup mushrooms, sliced
2 tomatoes, chopped and drained
1/8 tsp cayenne pepper
Hot sauce or chili sauce to taste
Salt and pepper to taste

Spray a large pan and heat over medium high. Add the onions and turmeric and cook for 3-5 minutes, until onions are soft, and turmeric is fragrant. Add the garlic and cook for 1 minute.

Add the remaining ingredients, except salt and pepper.

Stirring frequently, sauté for 6-8 minutes, until the vegetables are done, and the tofu is lightly fried. Use a potato masher to mash the tofu a bit, so it becomes the consistency of "scrambled eggs". Add a dash of salt and pepper to taste.

Serve with Rise & Shine Potatoes, sliced avocado and salsa or in a Breakfast Burrito/Taco

Rise & Shine Potatoes

Serves 4

I had to call them something, and Breakfast Potatoes sounded so…literal.

Olive oil or canola spray
1 medium onion, cut in half and sliced
4 medium russet potatoes, scrubbed, cut in half lengthwise and sliced thin
1 small red or green pepper, cut in half, seeded and sliced thinly
1 tsp granulated garlic
1 tsp Italian herbs
Salt and pepper
A sprinkle of paprika
1 TBLS fresh parsley, finely chopped

Mise en place, which means prepare all the vegetables. Spray a large frying pan and heat over medium high. Add the onions and cook, stirring for about 5 minutes. Add the peppers and potatoes and sprinkle with granulated garlic, Italian herbs, pepper and a little salt, stir well. Cover and allow to cook untouched on medium high for 4 minutes. Stir and cover again for 4 minutes. Uncover and allow the potatoes to brown, stirring just so they won't burn. Taste and adjust seasoning. Garnish with a sprinkle of paprika and chopped parsley.

Serve with Veggie Tofu Scramble or with/in Breakfast Burritos.

Oats & Berries & Nuts

Serves 4

Oatmeal is a stick to your ribs breakfast that is really great for you in so many ways! Oats are a whole grain, naturally gluten free, but for those folks who have Celiac Disease it is important to buy oats that are guaranteed to be gluten free. It is not the actual oats that contain gluten, but oats can be cross contaminated in a packaging facility. Oats are loaded with lots of vitamins, minerals and antioxidants. Rich in soluble fiber, protein and good fats, oats are an excellent way to help balance blood sugar, promote healthy gut bacteria, drop cholesterol and manage weight. And, this oatmeal recipe comes out purple!

---

1 1/2 cups rolled oats
1/2 cup quick cook steel cut oats
1 cup fresh or frozen blueberries
1/4 cup raw pumpkin seeds
2 TBLS real maple syrup

4 cups water
1/3 cup slivered almonds
Cinnamon
Almond milk

In a pot, put the oats, berries, pumpkin seeds, maple syrup and water. (I use a dry measuring cup to measure the oats, berries and water, so technically it is a bit less than 4 cups of water, than if you used a wet measuring cup for the water…wink.). Bring to a boil, stirring. Reduce heat to medium low and cook stirring for about 5 minutes. When the water is absorbed spoon into individual cups or bowls, pour on a dollop of almond milk and top with about 1 TBLS slivered almonds and a sprinkle of cinnamon.

Avocado Toast with Tomatoes

Serves 2

This recipe is about as straight-forward as they come. Simple and delicious!

---

4 pieces whole grain/seed bread, toasted
1 ripe avocado
2 tomatoes, thickly sliced

1-2 TBLS parsley, finely chopped
Salt and pepper
Toasted pine nuts

While the bread is toasting, slice the tomatoes and sprinkle with a little salt and pepper. Cut the avocado in half and remove the pit. Place two pieces of toast of each plate. Carefully scoop out each avocado half with a big spoon keeping it intact, cut into thin slices and fan them out across the toast, or just scoop it out and spread it on the toast. Top each piece with two tomato slices and sprinkle with the parsley and toasted pine nuts.

Serve on its own or with Rise & Shine Potatoes on the side.

Morning Smoothies!

There is nothing so simple and delicious as a healthful smoothie for breakfast! The following recipes can be mixed and matched, just bearing in mind you want a good balance of protein, good fat and fruit/veggies. My friends, we are working on changing our taste buds, so these smoothies may not taste very sweet at first, but it is totally worth getting used to foods that are less sweet, because sugar is Poison! Sugar is the culprit of so many issues in our society. And, don't get any crazy ideas about artificial sweeteners, because they are worse! But, I promise, given half a chance your taste buds will change! You will be so amazed at the scrumptiousness of raw kale in a morning smoothie! If you are not Kale Savvy yet, or if you are downright Kale-ophobic, just go slowly and add a little bit at first. You will quickly see that the taste disappears in the smoothie. And, you can use spinach or what I really like is Power Greens that you can find at Costco or most other stores.

You will feel so good, not only physically but, in every way, knowing that you are giving your precious body Super Foods first thing in the morning!

Remember, your body is the Temple for your Soul. Let's treat ourselves with reverence!

Real Food Green and Purple Smoothie

Serves 2

Here's the deal, I am not going to give you twelve different Smoothie recipes. It is unnecessary. I am giving you three recipes to play with. If you want a different flavor, use different fruits! Use orange juice instead of almond or soy milk. Toss in one half of a roasted sweet potato, or spinach instead of kale. The main thing to remember is to get a lot of greens into your smoothies and the rest is up for negotiation.

---

1 BIG handful kale or spinach or
    power greens (about 2 cups)
1 heaping cup frozen blueberries
1 banana
1/4 cup raw nuts, pumpkin seeds, walnuts, almonds…
    your choice! Mix it up!

2 TBLS ground flax
2 cups almond, soy, coconut, rice, flax or hemp milk,
    Unsweetened and Unflavored
Add a little cold water if it is too thick
1 TBLS almond or peanut butter

Put the ingredients into a NutriBullet, Vitamix or blender in this order and blend well!

This will not be overly sweet, but the goal is to change our taste buds, and move past the sugar cravings! Remember, you are feeding your body what it needs: Nutrition!

Strawberry and Banana and Kale, Oh My!

Serves 2

I made this Smoothie for my kiddos most mornings and they NEVER knew they were drinking kale! Sometimes I would bake a sweet potato the night before and plop a big hunk of nutrition into their Smoothie! Sometimes children are…selective eaters, but we want them to get all the nutrients their bodies and brains need to thrive. So, be sneaky, if necessary!

---

1 small handful or big handful kale, ribs removed
    and chopped
1 banana

2 cups frozen strawberries
1/2 cup orange juice, no sugar added
1 cup almond milk, unsweetened

Put everything into the blender in order and GO! Feel free to add flax meal, peanut or almond butter or other fruits. The beauty of Smoothies is you can mix and match!

Chocolate Smoothie!

Serves 2

Bet you didn't see this coming! But, aren't you happy it's here? Just to be clear, this is a Chocolate Smoothie, and it is super healthy! Just a note about frozen bananas: Freeze Bananas! They are Awesome! They make your smoothies creamier and colder! Peel and cut bananas into large chunks, put into a Ziplock freezer bag, zip almost all the way and suck all the air out, then zip it up! Lay flat in the freezer.

Then one evening when you have a hankerin' for ice cream, you will have frozen bananas ready to make Banana Ice Cream! Life is Good!

---

1 BIG handful greens of your choice
1 large or 2 small bananas, frozen in chunks
1 cup frozen blueberries
1/8 cup raw pumpkin seeds
2 heaping TBLS flax meal
2 heaping TBLS cocoa powder

1 tsp vanilla
1 TBLS maple syrup
1 heaping TBLS peanut or almond butter
2 cups almond milk (or your choice of dairy free milk)
1 cup cold water

Put everything into the blender in order and blend until smooth. Enjoy!

Raspberry Scones

Makes 10 Scones

I got the basics of this recipe, from all places as the punch line in a political post!
The post was from Glenn Rockowitz, and I have no idea if it was his recipe.
I have Veganized it, of course, and these babies are delicious!

---

2 cups all-purpose flour, plus a bit for rolling out
1/4 cup plus 1 TBLS sugar
1 TBLS baking powder
Zest from 1 medium lemon
1/2 tsp salt
8 TBLS = 1 stick Earth Balance, cut into
    1/2 inch cubes and chilled

3/4 cup plus 1 TBLS plant based cream
    (I use TJ's Soy Creamer,
    and it works great!)
1 cup frozen raspberries, keep them frozen
    until they are called for

Preheat the oven to 400 degrees.

Combine the 2 cups of flour, 1/4 cup of sugar, baking powder, lemon zest and salt in a large bowl and whisk together, breaking up any lumps. Cut the Earth Balance into the flour mixture with a pastry blender until small, pea-sized pieces remain.

Lightly flour your work surface and rolling pin. Pour the 3/4 cup of plant based cream into the flour mixture, using your fingers to mix just until it starts to come together. It will not all be incorporated and it will be a sticky mound. Turn the dough out onto your lightly floured work surface and gently knead just until the dough holds together. Form the dough into a rough rectangle, with the long edge toward you. Roll the dough into an 8 x 10 inch rectangle, keeping the long edge toward you.

Take the raspberries from the freezer and evenly arrange them in a single layer over the lower two-thirds of the rectangle, and press them into the dough. Some of them may break. It's okay!

Holding on to the top one-third of the rectangle (the part without berries), fold the dough over one third, then over one third again. *Use a spatula or scraper if the dough sticks to your work surface.

Flour the rolling pin again and gently roll the dough into a 1-inch-thick block. Square the ends with your fingers. Slice the block of dough into 5 squares, cutting straight down, do not saw back and forth. Cut each square diagonally into two triangles.

Transfer the scones to a lightly floured plate and pop them in the freezer for 5 minutes.

Remove the scones from the freezer and transfer to a sprayed cookie sheet, about 2 inches apart. Brush a thin layer of plant based cream on each scone and sprinkle with a bit of sugar. Bake until golden brown, about 20 minutes. Let them cool on the cookie sheet for 5 minutes, then transfer to a wire rack to cool.

Hors d'Oeuvres

Eat Your Vegetables, Bitches

Hors d'Oeuvres

Baked Vegan Goat Cheese Puttanesca

Serves 4 - 6

Oh, Holy Cats, is this dish ever delicious! I have made this several times for Potluck Dinners where most of the people are not vegan, and it is always a winner! The flavors are spectacular together. If you are going to try to slip this in without telling non-vegan folks about the "goat cheese", just remember to tell them it contains nuts!

4 oz vegan goat cheese (*Recipe follows*)	1/4 cup dry white wine
1 TBLS olive oil	1 -14 oz. can of diced tomatoes, in juice
1 medium onion, chopped	3/4 cup pitted kalamata olives, cut in half, more if you like!
5 cloves of garlic, chopped	1 TBLS capers
1 TBLS dried Italian herbs	1/4 cup pine nuts
1/4 - 1 tsp red pepper flakes	Freshly ground pepper to taste

Preheat oven to 400 degrees

Heat the olive oil in a sauté pan. Add chopped onions and cook over medium heat for a few minutes until becoming translucent. DO NOT BROWN. Add garlic, herbs, red pepper flakes and wine. Cook for one minute on medium high heat. Add the tomatoes, kalamata olives, capers, pepper and cook, stirring occasionally for 10 minutes over medium low heat.

Meanwhile, place the goat cheese log in the center of a baking dish. Choose a dish that you want to serve in, because this will not transfer. When the puttanesca is done, pour over the goat cheese and sprinkle the pine nuts on top. Bake for 10-12 minutes.

Serve with your choice of good crackers or toasted baguette slices.

Eat Your Vegetables, Bitches

Vegan Goat Cheese

Makes about 1 cup

One of the biggest 'misses' when people become vegan (besides bacon, of course) is cheese. This recipe will satisfy your desire for a creamy cheese to spread on crackers, to put a dollop on a salad or in several recipes in this book.

1/2 cup raw cashews, soaked
1/2 cup raw macadamia nuts, soaked
1 TBLS raw apple cider vinegar
1/4 cup lemon juice

1 TBLS miso
1/2 tsp salt
Water for blending

Soak the nuts for 12 hours in room temperature water, drain and rinse. If you don't have 12 hours you can bring a pot of water to a rolling boil, remove from heat and add the nuts. Cover and allow to sit for 30 minutes, drain and rinse.

Into the blender, add the nuts, apple cider vinegar, lemon juice, miso and salt. Add a smidge of water and blend. Add a little water if necessary for a smooth consistency. Not too much! Be patient, as the blending process can take a few minutes. Transfer to a covered mason jar and put it into a warm dark place for 24 hours. If you added too much water, you can strain through cheese cloth. The "Cheese" will get firm in the fridge, after the initial 24 hours.

*You can add fresh chopped herbs for a lovely herbed "cheese" spread…YUM!

Sweet Caramelized Figs with Vegan Goat Cheese

Makes 12 appetizers

If you are going to take the time to make homemade vegan goat cheese, I
better put more than one recipe in this book!

---

6 figs, cut in half lengthwise
2 TBLS Earth Balance
1 teaspoon olive oil
2 TBLS real maple syrup
2 TBLS balsamic vinegar
2-3 ounces vegan goat cheese *(Hors d'oeuvres)*
Salt and plenty of fresh coarsely ground pepper
1 baguette
olive oil

Preheat oven to 375 degrees.

Slice the baguette into 12 – half inch slices. Lightly brush each slice with olive oil and arrange on a baking sheet in a single layer. Bake for about 8 minutes at 375, until golden brown, turning once. Remove from the oven.

Meanwhile, wash the figs in cool water and dry with a paper towel. Cut off the stem, set the fig on its bottom and cut in half straight down. In a sauté pan large enough to hold all the figs, melt the Earth Balance and 1 tsp olive oil together over medium high heat. Reduce heat to medium and add the maple syrup, balsamic vinegar and stir, then add the figs cut side down and sauté for 2 minutes. Turn the figs over and add a little bit of salt and a lot of freshly ground black pepper. Allow the figs to cook for about 2-3 minutes more. Save the balsamic/maple syrup that is left in the pan.

On a cookie sheet lined with parchment paper or lightly sprayed, put the sautéed figs and top with a tsp of vegan goat cheese.

Bake in a 375 degree oven for about 5 minutes, or until the cheese begins to bubble and turn golden. Place one fig half on each toasted baguette slice and drizzle each with a bit of the leftover balsamic from the sauté pan.

Serve with pride!

Awesome Guacamole

Serves 6

Okay, I admit it, I have always gotten compliments on my Awesome Guacamole.
That's what the people say, "This Guacamole is Awesome!" Such a simple crowd pleasing dish!

---

3 medium avocados, ripe but not too soft
1 small red onion, chopped
2 Roma tomatoes or 1 large tomato, diced

1 clove garlic, pressed
1 lime, juiced, (or more)
Salt and pepper

Cut the avocados open lengthwise. Keep one of the pits. Scoop out the insides into a bowl and mash, leaving some chunks. Toss the pit into the avocado. This will keep it from turning brown. (wink) Add the onions, tomatoes and garlic. Stir. Squeeze half of the lime over the guacamole and add a little salt and a good pinch of pepper. Stir, taste and add more lime if you like. I like a lot of lime in my guacamole! Garnish with lime wedges.

Serve with tortilla chips or embody your Inner Millennial and spread it on a piece of toast! However you serve it, it is Awesome Guacamole!

Kale Chips

Serves 2 - 4

4 cups kale leaves
1 TBLS olive oil, plus a little more for your hands
1 1/2 TBLS Nutritional Yeast
1/2 tsp granulated garlic

1/4 tsp cumin
1/4 tsp chili powder
1/8 tsp cayenne
Salt

Preheat the oven to 275 degrees and line a baking sheet with parchment.

Remove the leaves from the kale stalk. Take the end in one hand and pull the leaves off up the stalk. Rip the kale into big pieces then wash and dry the leaves with a salad spinner. The kale must be dry.

Put the leaves into a large bowl and drizzle with 1/2 the olive oil and "massage" into the leaves with your fingers. Combine all the seasonings well. Sprinkle 1/2 the seasonings and massage the leaves. Add the remaining olive oil and sprinkle the remaining seasonings and mix well.

Arrange the kale leaves on the baking sheet in a single layer.

Bake at 275 degrees for about 20 minutes, stirring several times during cooking.

Do not overcook. Enjoy!

Veggie Boats

Makes about 12 - 14

Simple, beautiful and delicious!

Endive, Butter Lettuce or Romaine Leaves,
    washed and separated
1/2 cup red and/or green peppers, finely diced
1/2 cup zucchini, finely diced
1/2 cup red onion, finely diced
1/2 cup cucumber, peeled, seeded and diced

1/2 cup broccoli, finely chopped
1/2 cup olives, chopped
1 cup cooked quinoa
1/3 cup of your favorite salad dressing
    (Salad Dressings)

Toss the quinoa and veggies with the salad dressing. Load up each lettuce leaf, arrange on a pretty plate and enjoy!

   Eat Your Vegetables, Bitches

Hummus

Serves 4

For me, there is no Tabbouleh without Hummus. They go together like Spaghetti and vegan
Meatballs, Mashed Potatoes and Gravy, Peanut Butter and Jelly, you get the idea.
I like to spread Hummus on a cracker or pita then top it with Tabbouleh! Divine!

1 – 15 oz can chickpeas/garbanzo beans, drained	1/4+ cup olive oil
1-2 cloves garlic, chopped	2+TBLS vegetable broth for thinning
1/3 cup tahini	2 TBLS toasted pine nuts
Juice of 1 medium lemon (about 1/4 cup or more to your taste)	Paprika
1/2 + tsp salt	1 TBLS fresh parsley, finely chopped

Drain the chickpeas and rinse well in a colander. Into the blender or food processor put the chickpeas,
garlic, tahini, lemon, salt, olive oil and 2 TBLS vegetable broth. Process well until smooth, scraping
down the sides and adding more broth 1 TBLS at a time until your desired consistency is reached. The
Hummus should be thick and smooth. Taste and add more lemon or salt.

Turn the Hummus out onto a shallow bowl or a rimmed plate. Flatten the Hummus with a spoon,
making swirls. Drizzle with a little olive oil. Sprinkle with Paprika and parsley and scatter the pine
nuts on top!

Quinoa Tabbouleh ~ Gluten Free

Makes about 6 cups

I have so many great memories of working at Georgio's Ristorante in Studio City, California. The owners were from Lebanon, and I fell in love with the family and the amazing food they made for the family in the kitchen! Here is my version of Tabbouleh. It is gluten free, because gluten makes me feel cranky and brain foggy. This is dedicated to Mama, Joseph, Liza and Joe! And, all my pals with whom I worked. Thanks for the great memories!

---

1 bunch curly parsley
1 cup uncooked quinoa
4 green onions, diced
2-4 TBLS chopped fresh mint
1-2 cups diced fresh tomatoes, juice strained
1 lemon, juiced
1/4 cup extra virgin olive oil
Salt and freshly ground pepper

To cook the quinoa: Add 1 cup of rinsed quinoa to 2 cups of boiling water. Stir, turn heat down to low and cover. Check after 10 minutes. Cook until the water is absorbed. Fluff with a fork and cool.

Pick parsley leaves off and wash thoroughly ~ No Stems. Dry the parsley well. Chop the parsley very fine and put into a big bowl. Add one cup of completely cooled quinoa and mix gently. Add more quinoa to your liking. Find the parsley/quinoa combination that suits you!

Add green onions, mint and tomatoes. Add as much or as little of the tomatoes as your taste dictates. I like LOTS of tomatoes!

Juice the lemon and combine with the olive oil. Pour over the parsley mixture a little at a time, mixing to a consistency that is not too wet. You may not use it all. Add salt and pepper to taste.

You can play with this recipe adding more or less of any of the ingredients. Have fun with it!

Serve on a bed of lettuce dressed with a simple oil and vinegar and pita or with gluten free crackers, olives and hummus.

Roasted Garlic

This is a recipe that every cook should know how to make. It is so simple yet can turn ordinary food into something elegant and delicious!

You can make one head of garlic or 20! It can be refrigerated for up to two weeks or frozen for up to three months.

This recipe is for three heads of garlic.

---

3 heads garlic
1+ TBLS Olive oil

Preheat the oven to 400 degrees.

Peel most of the outside skin off the heads of garlic, leaving the head intact and the cloves connected.

Cut the tops off about ¼ inch to expose the tops of the cloves. Place the garlic on a big piece of foil.

Drizzle with olive oil, allowing the oil to drip down into the cloves.

Seal the foil around the garlic and bake for about 45 minutes on the center rack of the oven.

Pierce the center clove with a knife to make sure it is very soft. Depending on the size of the heads of garlic, you may need a little more roasting time. You can leave them in longer to turn golden brown and slightly caramelize.

Let the garlic cool a little before serving. Squeeze the bottom of a clove to push it out.

Serve with warm French or Italian bread or add to a variety of recipes in this book that call for garlic!

Crispy Baked Tofu

Serves 2

These little bites of scrumptiousness can be used in a variety of ways. On top of a salad, on top of stir-fry, in the Asian Tofu Bowl or make a peanut sauce and serve as an appetizer.

---

1 block firm tofu, drained well on paper towels	1 tsp ginger, finely chopped
2 TBLS Bragg's Liquid Aminos or Tamari or Soy Sauce	A pinch - 1/2 tsp cayenne pepper
1 1/2 TBLS sesame oil	4 TBLS water
1 tsp granulated garlic	1 TBLS cornstarch

In a small bowl combine the Bragg's, Tamari or Soy Sauce, sesame oil, granulated garlic, ginger, cayenne, water and whisk well. Cut the tofu into 1 inch chunks. Place the tofu chunks in a large Ziplock bag and pour the marinade over the tofu. Shake gently to coat. Release as much air as possible and Zip it well! Put the Ziplock in a baking dish so it lays flat. Refrigerate for at least one hour or overnight. Flip the bag periodically.

Preheat the oven to 375 degrees.

Spray a baking sheet. Drain the marinade, put the marinated tofu in a bowl and sprinkle with the cornstarch, and toss to coat well. Arrange the tofu in one layer on the baking sheet. Bake for 40 minutes, flipping each piece once halfway through baking. It should be golden brown and crispy!

Serve immediately!

Green Things, Yellow Things, Red Things, Orange Things
AKA: Vegetables

Eat Your Vegetables, Bitches

Green Things, Yellow Things, Red Things, Orange Things AKA: Vegetables

Vegetables: these are the REAL foods that we want at the forefront of our diet. And remember, I don't mean diet as in restriction, abstinence, off limits type of diet. When I use the word diet, I mean what you are putting in your mouth for sustenance, nutrition, to feed your cells, your body, your brain and your soul!

Your Grandmother and all the ancestors that came before us were correct; You are what you eat! So, we fill our plates with vegetables. Because Veggies need to lead!

Ratatouille

Serves 4

This is a crowd pleaser! Ratatouille is so versatile, it can be served as a side dish, over pasta, over zucchini noodles over brown or cauli-rice , on top of grilled polenta or with a side of mashed potatoes! You really cannot go wrong with Ratatouille!

---

1 TBLS olive oil
1 small eggplant
2 zucchinis
1 large onion
1 red pepper
1 yellow pepper

2 cups mushrooms
1 - 14 oz. can organic diced tomatoes
3 cloves garlic, chopped
Salt and pepper
1 TBLS Italian herbs (oregano, basil, rosemary, thyme)
    about 1 tsp each if adding separately

Chop all veggies into 1inch chunks. Heat 1 TBLS olive oil in a large skillet over medium high heat. Toss in the veggies (not the garlic) and cook until they begin to soften, about 5 minutes. Add the garlic and cook for one minute stirring. Add the can of tomatoes, stir in the herbs and salt and pepper and cover. Stir every 10 minutes for 30 minutes. The veggies should be soft.

Brussels Sprouts Extraordinaire

Serves 4

Who doesn't love Brussels Sprouts? Lots of people, that's who!
So, we make them so flavorful and delicious that the haters cannot hate.

---

1 lb. Brussels Sprouts, washed, trimmed and cut in half lengthwise	2 cloves garlic, pressed
1 TBLS olive oil	1 tsp dried thyme
1 large shallot, diced (about 1/3 cup)	salt and freshly ground pepper
	1/4 cup dry white wine

Heat the olive oil in a large sauté pan. Add the shallots and cook stirring for five minutes over medium heat. Add the garlic and cook for one minute. Add the Brussels Sprouts, thyme, salt and pepper and cook stirring for about 6-8 minutes or until the Brussels Sprouts begin to brown. Add the white wine, stir and cover. Allow them to cook for about 5 minutes. Check for doneness. You want the firm but soft.

Roasted Sweet Potatoes, Caramelized Onions, Vegan Goat Cheese and Kale

Serves 6

There is nothing like the smell and taste of caramelized onions in any dish!
But add roasted sweet potatoes and vegan goat cheese? This is delicious as it is, but add kale sautéed with garlic…Yup…that's what I'm talkin' about! This dish is great for a Holiday meal.

---

3 TBLS olive oil (divided)
3 lbs. Sweet Potatoes, peeled and cut
    into 1inch cubes
1 TBLS orange zest
4 TBLS orange juice
1 TBLS honey or maple syrup

1 large onion, peeled, cut in half and sliced
4 TBLS panko breadcrumbs
    (Or GF breadcrumbs)
3 ounces vegan goat cheese. *(Hors d'oeuvres)*
1 tsp dried thyme
Salt and freshly ground pepper

Preheat the oven to 450 degrees.

Toss the sweet potatoes in a large bowl with 2 TBLS olive oil, salt and pepper. Spray two cookie sheets with olive oil or canola spray. Spread the sweet potato chunks out in a single layer on two cookie sheets and roast for 10 minutes on separate racks.

While the potatoes are roasting, in the same large bowl whisk together the orange juice, orange zest and the honey.

Remove the potatoes from the oven and put them into the large bowl with the OJ mixture, toss to coat, spread them back onto the cookie sheets and roast another 10 minutes.

While the sweet potatoes are roasting, heat 1 TBLS of olive oil in a sauté pan and add the onions. Cook over medium heat, stirring occasionally for about 15 minutes, or until they begin to turn golden brown.

When the sweet potatoes are done, remove from oven and reduce the heat to 375 degrees. In a shallow 9 x 13 inch casserole dish, sprayed so the food will not stick, layer the potatoes, onions, panko breadcrumbs and vegan goat cheese, in that order.
Bake for 15 minutes.

For an added nutrient *BAM*, sauté 4-6 cups of kale, 2-4 cloves of chopped garlic and a little salt and pepper in 1 TBLS olive oil until tender. Serve the sweet potato dish on top of the kale!

Zucchini Noodles Aglio e Olio

(Garlic & Olive Oil)
Serves 2 as a Main Course or 4 as a side dish

May I just say, I love The Spiralizer! Someone was thinking when they said,
"Hey, let's make noodles out of Zucchini!"
However, here are some dos and don'ts to Spiralizing:

- Choose firm zucchini, not over or under ripe.
- Do not peel the zucchini.
  Not only does it look beautiful with the peel on, and pack more nutrition, but also the peel keeps the zucchini from "sweating" out unwanted liquid into your dish!
- Never salt zucchini before or during cooking.
  Salt causes the moisture in the zucchini to release, which will result in a mushy, soggy mess.
- Do not overcook.
  These are noodles! Cook them al dente!

---

5 large zucchinis
1-2 TBLS extra virgin olive oil
6 cloves garlic, slivered
A pinch to 1/2 teaspoon (or more) crushed red pepper
1/4 cup parsley, chopped
1/2 cup vegan Parmesan cheese, grated
2 TBLS pine nuts, toasted
A little salt & freshly ground pepper

Wash the zucchini and cut off the ends and cut in half crosswise. Place the zucchini in the Spiralizer set to thinish noodles and GO! Set aside on paper towels to drain.

Meanwhile, in a cold sauté pan add the slivered garlic, olive oil and crushed red pepper. Turn heat on to medium and keep the garlic moving for about two minutes. Do not let the garlic brown. Add the zucchini noodles to the garlic and olive oil and sauté for about 3 or 4 minutes, stirring frequently. At the very end, add salt and pepper to taste, then parsley. Toss quickly and turn onto a serving plate. Sprinkle with vegan parmesan cheese and toasted pine nuts.

Serve immediately.

Spiralized Sweet Potatoes with Garlic and Herbs

Serves 4

The juxtaposition of the sweet in the sweet potatoes and the
BAM of garlic and cumin makes for a complex flavor explosion!

---

1 TBLS olive oil
1 TBLS Earth Balance
1 medium onion, cut in half and thinly sliced
2 large or 4 medium sweet potatoes, washed and peeled
4-5 cloves garlic, minced

1 tsp dried thyme
1 1/2 tsp cumin
Salt and pepper
2 TBLS fresh parsley, finely chopped

Wash and peel the sweet potatoes. Run them through the Spiralizer. In a large sauté pan heat the olive oil and Earth Balance. Toss in the onions and allow to cook for about 10 minutes on medium heat. When the onions are starting to brown toss in the garlic, thyme, cumin and sweet potatoes. Stir well to combine with the onions, cover and cook for about 6 or 7 minutes or until the sweet potatoes are tender. Season with a little salt and a good pinch of pepper. Sprinkle with chopped parsley.

This is a wonderful Holiday side dish.

Lemony Broccoli

Serves 4

My favorite! What can I say…there is nothing like the simple flavors of broccoli and lemon.
Add a little garlic and some spice and watch out!
So simple, so delicious!

---

6 cups broccoli florets
1 TBLS olive oil
2 cloves garlic, pressed

1/2 or more of a lemon, juiced
Pinch red pepper flakes (optional)
A little salt and pepper

Bring a pot of water to boil. Add the broccoli and blanch for 2 minutes. The broccoli will be bright green and still crisp. Drain and rinse in cool water to stop the cooking. Shake off the excess water.

In a large sauté pan add the olive oil, garlic and red pepper. Turn heat on to medium high and cook for one minute. Add the broccoli and toss for one minute. Reduce heat to medium and add the lemon juice, salt and pepper and stir for one minute.

Serve immediately.

Roasted Broccoli

Serves 4

Something wonderful happens to Broccoli when it is roasted.
There is nothing boring about it. Give it a try and see how you like it!
You can use this same recipe for Asparagus, Brussels Sprouts, and Cauliflower, as well.

---

6 cups broccoli florets
2 TBLS olive oil
2 garlic cloves, pressed

1/4-1 tsp crushed red pepper (optional)
Salt and pepper

Preheat the oven to 425 degrees.

Combine the olive oil and garlic (crushed red pepper, if using) in a small bowl. Put the broccoli florets in a big bowl and pour the olive oil mix evenly over the broccoli. Toss really well to coat all of the broccoli. Spread evenly on a sprayed baking sheet and roast for 20 minutes without stirring, until becoming golden around the edges. Sprinkle with salt and pepper, to your liking.

Serve hot or warm.

Veggie Garlic Sauté

You can make this dish for 2 or 4, just add more veggies

Oh, how I love super simple, yummy dishes! This one is so good, and easy!
The beauty of this recipe is you can combine whatever vegetables
you have on hand and make a delicious dinner.

Slice and or chop onions, zucchini, broccoli, celery, carrots, cabbage, tomatoes, squash, mushrooms, cauliflower, spinach, eggplant…Really, whatever combo strikes your fancy!

Sauté in a little olive oil and a little toasted sesame oil over medium high heat for about 3 or 4 minutes, then add a good squirt of Karam's Garlic Sauce, a sprinkle of Italian herbs, salt and pepper to taste. *Let's talk about Karam's Garlic Sauce. This is a little known, but easily found Lebanese GEM for your kitchen. It is a sauce made from garlic, lemon and salt and will send your tastebuds soaring! You can find it in most major grocery stores in the refrigerated section.

Top with a sprinkle of Gomasio! Serve over pasta, brown rice, Cauli-Rice *(On the Side)* or just in a big bowl on its own!

"Buttery" Dill Carrots

Serves 4

I heard my friend Kim Bogan Goldman say something about Buttery Dill Carrots about twenty-five years ago. It sounded so yummy that I had to create a recipe. I am not sure if this is what Kim was talking about, but these are delicious. Blanching the carrots for two minutes before sautéing will bring out a bright orange color and help them to cook evenly.

---

1 pound carrots, washed, peeled and sliced
2 TBLS Earth Balance
2 cloves garlic, pressed

1 TBLS dried dill or 2 TBLS fresh dill, finely chopped
Salt and pepper

Wash, peel and slice the carrots. Bring a pot of water to boil, add the sliced carrots and blanch for two minutes. Drain well. In a large sauté pan heat the Earth Balance over medium high heat. Toss in the carrots and cook stirring well to coat with the Earth Balance for about 5 minutes. Add the garlic and cook stirring for 1 minute. Add the dill and stir to combine. Reduce heat to medium, cover and cook for about 5 minutes. Sprinkle with a little salt and pepper, to your liking.

Serve with Cabbage Rolls, Indian Lentil Curry or Grilled Tofu *(Main Courses)*.

Persian Green Beans

Serves 4

These babies cook longer than I would normally cook most vegetables,
but the flavors really get into the green beans and create Middle Eastern Magic!
You want to use very ripe tomatoes for the most flavor.
If your tomatoes are not ripe, or you don't have tomatoes on hand, use canned diced tomatoes.

---

1 TBLS olive oil
1 large onion, chopped
1 pound green beans, trimmed and cut in half
5 cloves garlic, chopped

1/4-1 tsp crushed red pepper
4 medium sized tomatoes, diced (about 3 cups)
    OR 1 1/2 – 14 ounce cans diced tomatoes
Salt and pepper

Trim the ends from the green beans and cut in half. Heat the olive oil in a sauté pan over medium high heat. Add the onions and cook stirring until they begin to brown. Reduce heat to medium, add the green beans and stir, cooking until the green beans begin to wilt, about 3-4 minutes. Add the garlic and crushed red pepper, stir. Cover and reduce the heat to low and simmer for 15 minutes. Stir every few minutes.

Add the tomatoes, salt and pepper and stir to combine. Cover and allow to simmer over low heat for about 10 minutes.

Serve with brown rice, Cauli-Rice *(On the Side)*, salad…Yum!

Baked Greek Veggies

Serves 4

This is such a simple and delicious dish that can be paired with
rice pilaf and a salad for an elegant peasant dinner!

---

2 zucchini, sliced
1 small eggplant, peeled and cubed
2 tomatoes, diced

1 onion, cut in half and sliced into strips
1/4 cup Greek Vinaigrette *(Salad Dressings)*
2 TBLS pine nuts

Prepare the Greek Vinaigrette.

Place all the veggies in a shallow baking pan and drizzle the vinaigrette over the veggies, stir and refrigerate. Allow to marinate for at least 1 hour.

Preheat the oven to 400 degrees. Bake the veggies on a sprayed cookie sheet for about 15 minutes, stir and bake another 10 - 15 minutes.

Sprinkle with pine nuts and serve with vegan Tzatziki *(Sauces and Such)* and Rice Pilaf *(On the Side).*

Veggie Fried Cauli-Rice

Serves 4

Fried Rice with a mega nutritional twist!

8 cups riced cauliflower
1 TBLS olive oil
1 TBLS toasted sesame oil
1 onion, chopped
2 garlic cloves, pressed
1 zucchini, chopped
1/2 cup red pepper, chopped

1/2 cup green pepper, chopped
1 cup broccoli coarsely chopped
1/2 cup sliced celery
1/2 to 1 cup sliced mushrooms
1-2 TBLS Bragg's Liquid Aminos or Tamari Sauce
Asian, Spicy or Crispy Baked Tofu, if desired

Heat the oil in a large skillet over medium-high heat. Add the chopped onions and sauté until beginning to turn translucent. Add the garlic and stir well for one minute. Add cauli-rice, zucchini, peppers, broccoli, celery and mushrooms. Stir-fry until the rice begins to soften and turn golden, about 5-6 minutes.

Season with Liquid Aminos or Tamari.

Top with Asian, Spicy or Crispy Baked Tofu (*Main Courses & Hors d'Oeuvres*) and/or chopped green onions!

Sprinkle with Gomasio.

Main
Courses

Main Courses

Eat Your Vegetables, Bitches

Mushroom Daube Provençal

Serves 4

Back in the day I made this recipe with beef. The chewy texture of the mushrooms and the red wine satisfy my desire for a saucy French dish.

2 TBLS olive oil
10 garlic cloves, crushed
24 ounces large mushrooms, quartered or thickly sliced (you choose!)
1 1/2 cups yellow onion, chopped
1 1/4 cup dry red wine
2 cups carrots, diced
1 cup celery, chopped
1 1/2 cups vegetable broth
1 TBLS tomato paste
1 TBLS fresh rosemary, chopped
1 TBLS fresh thyme, chopped
A dash ground cloves
1 cup diced tomatoes and juice
1 bay leaf
A little salt and a good pinch of pepper
1 TBLS chopped fresh thyme for garnish

In a Dutch oven, heat the olive oil over low heat. Add the garlic and cook stirring for about 5 minutes until the garlic is fragrant. Remove the garlic with a slotted spoon and set aside. Bring the heat up to medium-high. Add the mushrooms and onions and cook stirring occasionally for about 6-7 minutes. You want to brown the mushrooms and make them a little crusty. Add the wine and bring to a boil, scraping up any bits on the bottom. Add the garlic, carrots, celery, vegetable broth, tomato paste, rosemary, thyme, cloves, diced tomatoes, bay leaf, salt and pepper. Bring to a boil. Reduce heat to low and cover. Cook for 45 minutes. Discard the bay leaf and serve over mashed potatoes or mashed cauliflower or a combo of both, salad and crusty French bread.

Garnish with fresh chopped thyme.

CauliFlower Steaks with Pomodoro Sauce

Serves 4

This is a beautiful, delicious and nutritious dish that will impress your family and friends!
A heads up about cutting cauliflower into "steaks": sometimes there is a lot of "room" inside the head of cauliflower, and the steaks come out small. It's all good! Instead of one Big steak on a plate you have two or three small steaks. Don't sweat it! It will be scrumptious.
Sprinkle some chopped parsley on the finished plate and you have a beautiful masterpiece!

2 TBLS olive oil (divided)
1 large head cauliflower, quartered then sliced about 1/2 inch thick
1 medium onion, cut in half and sliced
3 cloves garlic, pressed
3 cups sliced mushrooms (or more!)
Salt and pepper
4 cups Pomodoro Sauce *(Sauces and Such)*
2 TBLS fresh parsley, chopped
Vegan mozzarella or parmesan (optional)

In a large sauté pan, heat 1 TBLS of the olive oil over medium high heat. Reduce heat to medium and add the onions, stirring until they start to become translucent, about 5 minutes. Add in the garlic and stir to combine. Toss in the mushrooms and stir. Cover and cook about 3 minutes. Remove the lid, sprinkle with a little salt and pepper and stir to combine. Remove the onions, garlic and mushrooms to a plate.

Add 1 TBLS olive oil to the same sauté pan over medium high heat.

Add the cauliflower "steaks" and sprinkle with salt and pepper. Reduce the heat to medium. Cover the pan and allow them to cook for about 5 minutes.

Turn the "steaks" over and sprinkle this side with a little salt and pepper and cook for about 3-5 minutes. You want the "steaks" to brown.

Heat the Pomodoro Sauce. Ladle a big scoop of Pomodoro Sauce onto each plate, lay the Cauliflower Steak on the sauce and top with a big spoonful of the onions and mushrooms. Top with a dollop of Pomodoro Sauce, vegan cheese if using and a sprinkle of parsley.

Eat Your Vegetables, Bitches

Eggplant Lasagna

Serves 6

Here is another crowd pleaser! I know I have a winner when my meat and potatoes people rave about a dish! This is one of those!

2 large eggplants, peeled and sliced lengthwise 3/4-inch thick
3 TBLS olive oil (divided)
Salt and freshly ground black pepper
2-3 cups sliced mushrooms, your choice of variety (I like a lot of mushrooms!)
2 TBLS garlic, minced
2 tsp dried thyme
2 cups vegan ricotta *(Recipe follows)*
2 flax eggs
1 cup grated vegan mozzarella
1 tsp dried oregano
2 TBLS freshly chopped parsley
4 cups Pomodoro Sauce *(Sauces and Such!)*

Preheat oven to 400 degrees

Arrange sliced eggplant in a single layer on 2 sheet pans. Brush on both sides using 2 tablespoons of olive oil and season with salt and pepper. Roast the eggplant until it is soft and golden, about 25 minutes.

You will need two cookie sheets. Place them off center to each other in the two center racks. Turn slices halfway through and, rotate the cookie sheets, the top rack goes to the bottom rack, bottom to the top rack.

Meanwhile, in a large skillet add the remaining 1 tablespoon of oil and heat over medium high. Add the sliced mushrooms. Sauté until soft for about 5 minutes. Add the minced garlic and thyme. Cook for another 2 minutes. Once the mushrooms are cooked remove and set aside to cool.

In a large bowl add the vegan ricotta, flax eggs *(Sauces and Such)*, 1/4 cup vegan mozzarella, oregano, parsley, mushrooms, 1 teaspoons of salt and 1/2 teaspoon pepper. Mix well.

Reduce heat in oven to 350 degrees. Brush a 9x13 inch baking dish with oil, or spray with canola or olive oil spray.

Spread half of the Pomodoro sauce on the bottom of the prepared baking dish. Lay half of the eggplant slices on top of the sauce followed by the ricotta mixture. Lay the remaining slices of eggplant and finish with Pomodoro sauce. Top with the vegan mozzarella. Bake at 350 degrees for 30 minutes until golden brown. Allow to rest for 5 minutes before serving.

Vegan Ricotta

About 2 cups

If you are an Italian food lover like me, you will appreciate this simple and scrumptious Ricotta recipe! Cheese is a Big miss for a lot of people when they go plant based, but it doesn't have be gone forever! Use this recipe for lasagna, manicotti or stuffed shells. Buon appetito!

2 cups raw cashews, soaked
2/3+ cup water
3 cloves garlic, pressed
2 1/2 TBLS nutritional yeast

1 large lemon, juiced
1 tsp salt
1/2 tsp pepper

Soak the raw cashews in a bowl of cold water for 2 hours. If you do not have 2 hours to spare, you can boil a small pot of water, remove from heat, add the cashews and soak them for 30 minutes.

Drain the cashews and put all the ingredients into a food processor or blender. Process until the mixture resembles ricotta, scraping down the sides to keep it moving. It should be rather thick, smooth and creamy. Add additional water, if necessary, to keep the mixture moving in the blender or food processor.

This will keep in the refrigerator for 5-6 days.

Cabbage Rolls

Serves 4

Peasant food…I love it! Simple and delicious. I make this recipe with cauli-rice for an extra dose of nutrients. No one will know the difference and everyone's cells will vibrate with joy!

---

1 medium head green cabbage,
    washed, cored and steamed
Olive oil spray
1 package TJ's Beefless Ground Beef
2 cups Cauli-Rice or cooked jasmine rice

1 medium onion, chopped
2 cloves garlic, chopped
1 1/2 TBLS Italian herbs
Salt and pepper
4 cups Pomodoro Sauce *(Sauces and Such)*

Remove two outer leaves, wash the cabbage and carefully remove the core with a knife, about 2-3 inches deep. In a large pot with 2-3 inches of water, place a steamer basket and steam the cabbage, core side down for about 20 minutes. Let cool.

Spray a sauté pan and cook the onion on medium high, stirring until translucent. Do Not Brown.

Add the Beefless Ground Beef breaking up with a fork as it cooks.

Add the Rice or Cauli-Rice, garlic, Italian Herbs, salt and pepper.

Add 2 cups of Pomodoro Sauce and stir to combine. Allow to simmer on medium low for 10 minutes.

Put the remaining Pomodoro Sauce in the bottom of a 9 x 13 inch baking dish.

Gently peel away cabbage leaves, trying not to break them. Fill each leaf, on the stem end, with a big spoonful of stuffing. Fold the sides in and roll up. Place the Cabbage Rolls seam side down in the baking dish. Cover with foil and bake at 350 degrees for 45 minutes.

Eat Your Vegetables, Bitches

Fiesta Pepper Tofu & Veggies

Serves 4

Whenever I created a recipe and it was delicious (which was often, hence the cookbook),
my Wasband used to say, "Did you write this down?"
This was one of the many recipes I wrote down.
Of course, all those years ago the recipe was Fiesta Pepper Chicken.
This is just as delicious, and no one died for our dinner!

1 box extra firm tofu, drained and diced into 1 inch cubes
2 TBLS olive oil
1 medium onion, chopped
5 cloves garlic, chopped
A dash crushed red pepper, more for spicy!
1 1/2 tsp Jerk Seasoning
Salt and pepper to taste
1 cup white wine
2 small or 1 large zucchini, cut into bite size cubes
1 red bell pepper, diced
1 green bell pepper, diced
2 cups mushrooms, sliced
1 14 oz. can diced tomatoes
1 tsp Vegetable Better Than Bouillon

I like to use a Wok for this recipe, because the tofu really gets to brown. Heat 1 TBLS olive oil over medium high heat and add the tofu. Allow the tofu to gently brown, shaking the pan every one minute or so. After about 4-5 minutes, or when the tofu has browned, add the onion. Cook stirring about 4 minutes.

Add the garlic, crushed red pepper and sprinkle the Jerk Seasoning, salt and pepper over the tofu and onions. Cook stirring for 1 minute on medium high. Stir in the wine, zucchini, peppers, mushrooms, tomatoes and Vegetable Better Than Bouillon. Cook over medium for 15 minutes, stirring every few minutes.

Serve over brown rice, Cauli-Rice *(On the Side)* or eggless noodles and a salad.

Mushroom Stroganoff

Serves 4

During the Coronavirus quarantine in March 2020 I did a lot of cooking at home, more than usual. One day I saw a box of Baby Portobello mushrooms in the fridge that needed to be cooked THAT DAY! So, I started creating. I used to love Beef Stroganoff and have missed those flavors of the tang of sour cream and the tiny nip of dill. This was a one shot creation. The Foodie in me knew exactly what to do. I hope you enjoy this one as much as my family does!

Olive oil or canola spray
1 medium onion, coarsely chopped
1 - 24 ounce box of Baby Portobello Mushrooms, cleaned, dried and thickly sliced
3 cloves garlic, finely chopped
1/2 cup dry red wine
1 tsp dried Italian herbs
2 tsp dried dill
2 cups vegetable broth
1 TBLS flour or corn starch
1 cup plain unsweetened dairy free yogurt or dairy free sour cream
    (Kite Hill Plain Almond Milk Yogurt is Da Bomb!)
1 TBLS lemon juice
Salt and pepper
Fresh parsley, chopped

Spray a large sauté pan and heat over medium high. Add the onions and cook for about 5 minutes allowing to get very golden brown. Add the mushrooms and continue cooking for another 3-5 minutes, stirring. When the mushrooms have a nice brown to them add the garlic and stir for 1 minute. Add in the red wine and bring up the heat to high for 1 minute, scraping up any bits on the bottom of the pan. Reduce heat to medium and add the vegetable broth and herbs. Simmer uncovered for about 10 minutes.

Mix the flour or corn starch with a little water or broth and stir well. Stir into the pan and mix well. Allow to simmer for a few minutes until it begins to thicken.

Remove from heat and add the yogurt, lemon juice and pepper.

Taste and add salt, if necessary.

Sprinkle with chopped parsley.

Serve over eggless noodles, Mashed Cauliflower *(On the Side)*, rice, quinoa or Mashed Potatoes *(On the Side)*.

Eat Your Vegetables, Bitches

Roasted Pepper Curry with Spinach, Potatoes and Mushrooms

Serves 4

I love the flavor of roasted red peppers! The spices in this dish are sublime!

3 large red bell peppers
1 TBLS olive oil
1 red onion, diced
4 cloves garlic, chopped
1/4 – 1 teaspoon crushed red pepper
1 can coconut milk, about 1½ cups
2 TBLS red curry paste (or to taste)
2 TBLS cornstarch

1/2 tsp smoked paprika
2 cups mushrooms, sliced
1 1/2 cups potatoes, peeled and cut into
        1 inch chunks and boiled (not too soft)
OR 1 can chickpeas, drained
2 cups fresh spinach, chopped
1 cup cherry tomatoes, halved
A little salt and pepper

Preheat the oven to 425 degrees.

Roast (bake) the peppers on the top rack of the oven for about 30 minutes, until they are charred. Turn them halfway through the roasting time. Remove from oven and put them in a paper bag to sweat and cool, then remove and compost the skin, stems and seeds. Set the roasted peppers aside. Reduce heat to 375 degrees.

While the peppers are roasting, heat the olive oil and sauté the onions over medium heat until golden. Add in the garlic and crushed red pepper and stir for 1 minute. Season with salt and pepper and set aside.

In a food processor or blender mix the roasted red peppers, onion and garlic, coconut milk, red curry paste, cornstarch and smoked paprika until well combined. Taste and add more salt and pepper, if necessary.

Transfer the sauce to an oven safe skillet, and add the mushrooms, potatoes or chickpeas, spinach and tomatoes. Stir well. Bake at 375 for about 30 minutes.

Serve with brown basmati rice or Cauliflower Rice *(On the Side)*.

Easy Stir Fry

Serves 4

It is so easy to toss a variety of vegetables into a wok and call it dinner!

Olive oil or canola oil spray
2 TBLS sesame oil
1 box firm or extra firm tofu, drained well and cut into 1 inch chunks
1/2-1 TBLS Sriracha, optional
1 medium onion cut in half and sliced length wise into strips
1 red pepper cut in half and sliced length wise into strips
2 cups broccoli in small florets
1 cup carrots, peeled and sliced at an angle
1 cup celery cut into 1/2 inch pieces at an angle
1 cup snow peas
2 cups mushrooms, sliced
1/4 head cabbage, sliced into 1/2 inch strips
2-3 cloves garlic, pressed
1/2 -1 tsp crushed red pepper, optional
2-3 TBLS Tamari or Bragg's Liquid Aminos
2 TBLS Hoisin Sauce

Drain the tofu and press between lots of paper towels for a couple of minutes. Prepare all the vegetables.

Spray the wok or sauté pan. Add 1 TBLS of the sesame oil and turn heat on high. Before it starts to smoke, reduce heat to medium high and gently add the tofu, allowing to cook for one minute, shake it up to rearrange, and allow to cook again, until the tofu is lightly brown on most sides, about 5-6 minutes Add the Siracha and 1 TBLS Bragg's Liquid Aminos or Tamari and toss with the tofu. Remove the tofu from the wok.

Spray the wok again, add the other TBLS of Sesame oil and reheat the wok. Add all the veggies in order. Cover and allow the veggies to cook for 1 minute without stirring then give the wok a shake to loosen the veggies. With a big spoon stir the veggies and keep them moving until the broccoli is firm and bright green, about 2 minutes. Turn the heat to low. Push the vegetables to the outside making a space in the center of the wok. Add 1–2 TBLS Tamari or Bragg's, the 2 TBLS of Hoisin sauce and stir to combine. Stir the vegetables into the sauce and cook over high heat for one minute. Spoon some rice, then the stir-fry into big bowls and top with the tofu!

*Make it Chow Mein by adding cooked spaghetti to the Stir Fry!

Eat Your Vegetables, Bitches

Eat Your Vegetables, Bitches

CauliWally Tacos

Makes about 12 tacos

I was checking out at Trader Joe's one day, chatting with the checkout guy, and he mentioned he was getting ready to go on his lunch break and was looking forward to Cauliflower and Walnut Tacos. You can imagine how my ears (and salivary glands) perked up!
I went back into the store and bought a cauliflower, went home and began to create!
These are South of the Border Badass!

Olive Oil or Canola Spray
1 medium onion, chopped
3 cloves garlic, chopped
1 small head of cauliflower, cut into florets and shredded in a food processor or finely chopped
1 cup walnuts, finely chopped – measure before chopping
2 TBLS chili powder (heaping)
1 TBLS cumin (heaping)
1 TBLS dried Italian herbs
1/2 - 1 chipotle pepper in adobo sauce, finely chopped (If you don't like too much spice start with
        1/4 of a chipotle pepper)
1 medium tomato, finely chopped
1/4- 1/2 cup vegetable broth
Juice of 1/2 a lime or more
Salt and pepper to taste
12 corn tortillas
Your favorite taco fixins'

Spray a large sauté pan well. Add the onion and cook stirring over medium heat until onions begin to turn golden. Add the garlic and stir for 1 minute. Add the cauliflower, walnuts, chili powder, cumin, herbs, chipotle pepper, tomato, vegetable broth and lime. Bring to a good simmer stirring well to combine, then reduce heat to medium low and cover for 15 minutes, stirring every 3-4 minutes. Taste and add salt or more chipotle, if desired.

Serve in crispy taco shells with lettuce, tomato, salsa and avocado slices or guacamole, or "fired" corn tortillas with all of your favorite fixins'. May I suggest Spicy Cabbage Slaw *(Salads and Whatnot)*!
"Fired" Corn Tortillas – Over a medium flame on a gas stove, place a corn tortilla on the flame and turn every 10 seconds or so. Keep turning until desired crispness and char is achieved!

Eat Your Vegetables, Bitches

Veggie Fajitas

Serves about 4

I ordered Vegetable Tacos from this little place in Ballard on Christmas Eve 2018, and they were delicious! I have recreated them here. In Tex-Mex, Fajita refers to skirt steak, but we will just call this a misnomer and go from there, okay?

1 medium red pepper, seeded and sliced in strips
1 medium yellow or orange pepper, seeded and sliced in strips
1 medium yellow onion, cut in half and sliced in strips
1 large zucchini, cut into 3 chunks and sliced into sticks
3 TBLS Balsamic Vinegar
1 TBLS cumin
1 tsp granulated garlic
1 TBLS water
1 tsp black pepper
1 TBLS olive oil
12 Corn Tortillas
4 cups shredded cabbage
1 cup red onion, thinly sliced
1 avocado, sliced

Sauce:
3/4 cup Vegan Mayo
1 clove garlic, pressed
1-3 TBLS Sriracha (depending on how much spice you like!)
3-4 TBLS lime or lemon

Slice the peppers, onions and zucchini and put into a large Ziplock.

Whisk together the Balsamic Vinegar, cumin, granulated garlic, water and black pepper. Pour over the veggies. Shake the bag to coat. Allow to marinate for at least one hour in the refrigerator. Turn the bag over every 15 minutes.

For the Sauce: Stir all the ingredients together. Add more lime or lemon to taste. Refrigerate while you make the fajitas.

Heat the olive oil over high in a cast iron skillet or another heavy skillet. When very hot add the veggies and sauté, stirring occasionally until the veggies begin to brown, about 5 minutes. Remove from heat.

Heat the tortillas over the flame of a gas stove or in the microwave for 20-30 seconds wrapped in paper towels. Fill the tortillas with veggies, cabbage, red onion and top with sauce. Serve with Black Beans, Spanish Rice , sliced avocado and limes on the side!

Stuffed Peppers

Serves 4 - 6

I love creating traditional dishes that were made with meat and revamping to make them vegan! And, blowing non-vegan folks out of the water with deliciousness!

---

4 bell peppers, any color
1 TBLS olive oil
1 medium onion, chopped
2 cups raw "riced" cauliflower OR 2 cups cooked brown or white rice (not sticky rice)
2 cups sliced mushrooms
3 cloves garlic, pressed
1/4 - 1 tsp crushed red pepper, optional
1 TBLS dried oregano
1 TBLS dried basil
1 package TJ 's Beefless Ground Beef (Trader Joe's)
1 14oz. can crushed tomatoes (if Diced Tomatoes put through a blender)
1/3 cup pine nuts
Salt and pepper
3 cups or more Pomodoro Sauce *(Sauces and Such)*

Preheat the oven to 350 degrees

Heat 1 TBLS of olive oil in a sauté pan over medium high heat. Add onion and cook stirring until translucent, about 4 minutes. Add the "riced" cauliflower or rice and mushrooms. Cook for about 5 minutes. Add the garlic, crushed red pepper and herbs. Stir well and push this mixture to the outside of the pan, leaving the center open. Add the Beefless Ground Beef, breaking up with a fork as it warms. Stir everything together and add the can of tomatoes, pine nuts, salt and pepper. Simmer on low about 10 minutes.

Wash and cut each pepper in half across the stem. Remove the insides including stems, seeds and fibers. Pour the Pomodoro sauce into a 9 x 13 inch baking pan. Over fill each pepper half with the stuffing mixture and lay them stuffed side down in the sauce. Cover with foil and bake for 40 minutes. Remove the foil and bake another 10 minutes or until the peppers are somewhat soft.

Serve with your favorite salad and crusty Italian bread.

Olivia's Favorite Pasta

Serves 4 - 6

My daughter, Olivia has always loved olives. We used to tell her that is why we named her Olivia. I can picture this adorable little girl with long blonde hair and an olive on each finger! This has always been her favorite pasta dish! You will soon see why!

1 TBLS olive oil
1 medium onion, cut in quarters and sliced
2 carrots, peeled and sliced
2 small zucchinis, sliced
2 cups mushrooms, sliced
1 bell pepper, sliced… red, green, yellow, orange…you choose!
1-2 cups broccoli florets
3 cloves garlic, pressed
1/4 to 1 tsp crushed red pepper
1 1/2 - 14.5 ounce cans diced tomatoes
1 TBLS dried Italian Herbs
1/2 cup dry white wine
3/4 cup of vegetable broth
3/4 cup + Kalamata Olives cut in half
Salt and freshly ground pepper
2 TBLS fresh chopped parsley
1 pound of fusilli or penne pasta, cooked to package directions

Prepare all the vegetables. Heat 1 TBLS of olive oil over medium high heat. Toss in the onions and cook, stirring for about 2 minutes. Add the carrots and cook for 3 minutes. Add the zucchini, mushrooms, peppers and broccoli and cook over medium heat for 3 minutes, until the broccoli starts to turn bright green, stirring. Push the veggies aside and make a space in the middle of the pan. Add a smidge more of olive oil, the crushed red pepper and garlic, stirring constantly so the garlic does not burn, about 30 seconds. Stir this evenly into the vegetables. Add the tomatoes, herbs, white wine, broth, olives and raise the heat to high for 1 minute, stirring all together. Reduce heat to low and simmer for about 10 minutes. Taste and add salt, if necessary. The olives are salty, so taste first!

Put the hot pasta in a big shallow pasta bowl, pour the vegetable sauce evenly over the top and sprinkle with chopped parsley. Toss and serve at the table! Your family and friends will be impressed!

Buon Appetito!

Portobello Mushroom Burgers

Makes 2

If you are a burger lover, whether or not you love mushrooms, this one will look you in the eye and say, "I'm your Huckleberry." If you don't get the Tombstone reference, that's okay. Just try these burgers and report back!

---

2 good size Portobello Mushrooms, wiped clean and gutted
2 TBLS balsamic vinegar
2 TBLS Bragg's Liquid Aminos or tamari or soy sauce
2 TBLS vegetable broth
1 clove garlic, pressed
1 tsp Italian herbs
pinch of salt
1/2 tsp pepper
1 TBLS olive oil
2 TBLS Madeira
Burger buns
Garlic Aioli *(Sauces and Such)*
Lettuce
Tomatoes
Pickles
Onions

Remove the stem and scrape out the black "gills" from the mushrooms. Save for vegetable broth or compost them. In a measuring cup (so you can pour) combine the balsamic, Bragg's, vegetable broth, garlic, Italian herbs, salt and pepper. Stir well. Put the Portobellos in a large Ziplock, pour the marinade over and zip it up! Gently shake the bag to cover the mushrooms and put in the refrigerator for 1 hour or up to 4 hours, turning over halfway through.

Put the 1 TBLS olive oil in a grill pan or cast iron skillet and heat on high until very hot but not smoking. Reduce heat to medium high and cook the mushrooms for about 5 minutes on each side, adding a little sprinkle of salt and pepper. Underside up, drizzle each mushroom with 1 TBLS Madeira. Allow to cook for 1 minute then turn over twice so the other side will soak up the wine.

Serve with all of your favorite toppings on a toasted burger bun. Excellent with a schmeer of Garlic Aioli *(Sauces and Such)*!

Eat Your Vegetables, Bitches

Carrot Dogs

Serves 4 - 6

Okay, I understand this sounds weird, to say the least. And I know my Texas family is laughing their butts off and shaking their heads at the thought of Carrot Dogs, but stay with me because I promise you won't be sorry! And, if you knew what went into traditional hot dogs, as my brother Bob says, "Lips and A#@holes"... trust me, you will love these!

6-8 large (a bit longer than hot dog sized) Carrots, peeled and ends cut off

Marinade:

1/4 cup vegetable broth
1/4 cup apple cider vinegar
3 TBLS Bragg's Liquid Aminos or Tamari
     or Soy Sauce
2 TBLS maple syrup or agave

2 tsp Liquid Smoke
1 TBLS Dijon mustard
1 heaping tsp minced garlic
1 TBLS pepperoncini or jalapeno or pickle juice
1 tsp Onion powder

Peel the carrots and cut off the ends, making a bit longer than the length of a hot dog bun.

Bring a big pot of water to boil. Add the carrots and boil for 10-12 minutes depending on the size of the carrots. JUST until fork tender! Don't overcook.

Drain and rinse twice in cold water, soaking for a few minutes in cold water to stop the cooking.

Drain well.

Put the carrots into a large Ziplock bag.

Combine all the marinade ingredients in a bowl and whisk well.

Pour the marinade over the carrots and Zip the bag closed.

Place the bag flat in a baking dish, so the carrots soak up the marinade. Refrigerate, turning the bag over every hour.

Marinate for 4-6 hours.

Grill the Carrot Dogs on the BBQ, basting as they cook. Grill until they are heated through and have grill marks. They can be cooked on the stove in a cast iron skillet or another heavy skillet.

Serve on a toasted Hot Dog bun with all your favorite condiments! So delicious with Dijon Mustard!

Vegan Baked Deliciousness

Serves 6

This is a wonderful casserole for parties and potlucks. It is Deliciousness! Hence the name!

"Meat Sauce"

1 TBLS Olive Oil	1 package Trader Joe's Beefless Ground Beef
1 yellow onion, chopped	1 tsp paprika
3 cloves garlic, pressed	1 TBLS ground cumin
1-14oz. can diced tomatoes	1 TBLS Italian herbs
1 small red bell pepper, chopped	3/4 cup vegetable broth
2 TBLS tomato paste	Salt and pepper

Heat the olive oil in a sauté pan over medium high heat. Add the onion and cook stirring until becoming golden brown.

Add the garlic and sauté for 1 minute stirring.

Add the diced tomatoes, tomato paste and red bell pepper and cook for 2 minutes.

Add the Beefless Ground Beef and stir well, breaking up as it cooks.

Add the remaining ingredients and stir well. Simmer on low for about 20 minutes, stirring a few times until the sauce starts to thicken.

Taste and adjust the seasonings, if necessary.

Remove from heat and set the sauce aside.

"Cheese Sauce"

2 cups Non Dairy Milk-like substance, unsweetened and unflavored (almond, soy, oat, hemp)	1/2 tsp turmeric powder
	1 TBLS olive oil
3-4 TBLS Nutritional Yeast	2 TBLS all-purpose flour or corn starch
1 heaping tsp granulated garlic	1 tsp Vegetable Better Than Bouillon
1 TBLS Earth Balance	

Add all the ingredients to a pot and whisk constantly over medium high heat for 3-5 minutes. Add more flour or corn starch, if it is not thick enough. Reduce the heat to medium low and cook for about two minutes, whisking. The consistency should be thick but pourable. Remove from heat and set aside.

"The Vegetables"
2 large zucchinis, cut into rounds a bit more than a 1/4 inch thick, raw
1 large eggplant, cut into rounds a bit more than a 1/4 inch thick and pre-baked at 350 degrees for 15 minutes

Preheat oven to 375 degrees.

Spray a 9x13 inch baking dish. Put half of the pre-baked eggplant slices in the bottom of the dish.

Top with half of the "meat sauce", spreading with a spoon, then add half of the zucchini slices and half of the "cheese sauce".

Do a second layer in the same order ending with the "cheese sauce".

Bake for 35-40 minutes until a bit golden. Remove from oven and allow to cool for 15 minutes before serving.

Eat Your Vegetables, Bitches

Veggie Pad Thai

Serves 4

I love Pad Thai! The spices combined with the hint of fresh basil and peanuts are spectacular.

For the Sauce

1/4 cup Bragg's Liquid Aminos or Tamari
    or Soy Sauce
4 TBLS smooth peanut butter
1 TBLS tamarind paste
1 TBLS sesame oil
1 TBLS olive oil

2 TBLS red curry paste
1 TBLS honey or maple syrup
Juice of 1 large lime
1 tsp or more Sriracha
    (makes this dish a 2 out of 5 stars)
    *omit the Sriracha if your curry paste is spicy.

1 – 10oz. package Pad Thai noodles
    (check cooking time)
Canola spray
1 TBLS sesame oil
1 TBLS olive oil
1/2 a medium yellow onion, sliced
3 garlic cloves, chopped
1 zucchini, cut in half length wise and sliced
1 medium carrot, peeled and thinly sliced

1 cup sliced mushrooms
2 cups broccoli florets
1/4 cup vegetable broth
3 TBLS peanuts, chopped
3 TBLS scallions, chopped
3 TBLS fresh basil,
    leaves rolled together and sliced
Lime wedges

In a medium size bowl combine the Bragg's, peanut butter, tamarind paste, sesame oil, olive oil, red curry paste, honey, lime juice, and Sriracha. Whisk well and set aside.

Set a big pot of water on to boil. When the water is boiling add the Pad Thai noodles, stir and turn off heat. Soak for 6 minutes. (Or cook by the package directions, if different) Meanwhile, spray the wok or sauté pan and add the TBLS of sesame oil and heat. Add all the veggies and sauté for 2-3 minutes. Don't overcook.

Test the noodles for doneness. Rinse the noodles very well in cold water and drain. You want to get all that starch off so they won't be sticky!

Pour the sauce and the 1/4 cup of vegetable broth over the veggies and stir. Add the noodles a handful at a time, stirring as you go, so you get the right ratio of noodles and saucy veggies. Combine well. Turn out onto a serving platter or into big shallow bowl. Garnish with chopped peanuts, basil ribbons, scallions and lime wedges!

Top with Crispy Baked Tofu, if you so desire *(Hors d'Oeuvres)*!

Serve immediately! This dish will become sticky if it sits.

Eat Your Vegetables, Bitches

Indian Lentil Curry

Serves 4 - 6

I love Indian food any way I can get it! This recipe is an easy way to have curry in a hurry!

---

1 1/2 cups of a mix of any dry lentils, rinsed
5 cups vegetable broth
3 TBLS yellow curry powder, mild or medium
1/2 tsp turmeric
2 tsp cumin
4 cloves garlic, chopped or pressed
1 tsp oregano
Salt and pepper to taste
1 small zucchini, diced
1 carrot, peeled and sliced
1 small onion, sliced
1 cup broccoli florets
OR
3 cups of frozen mixed vegetables

In a big pot bring to a boil the five cups of vegetable broth. Add the lentils and stir. Add the curry powder, turmeric, cumin, garlic, oregano, salt and pepper. Stir. Cover and cook on medium-low, stirring occasionally for about 40 minutes.

If you are using fresh, raw vegetables, add them to the pot after 25 minutes of cooking. If you are using frozen vegetables, add them in the last 5 minutes of cooking.

Taste and adjust the seasoning to your liking.

Serve with Yellow Coconut Rice *(On the Side)*, basmati rice, Cauli Rice *(On the Side)* or quinoa. Sriracha on the side.

Jackfruit Tacos

Serves 4

As a meat eater I loved pulled pork tacos! Enter the weird and wonderful Jackfruit!
A whole Jackfruit looks like a giant green mango with spikes. It is a strange looking fruit!
Then you crack it open and you have all these pockets of big kernels that you get to dismantle and weed through. There is a lot of sap, which makes cleanup…interesting. It is slimy and a LOT of work. But the good news is, Trader Joe's has canned Jackfruit in brine for about $1.99, which makes these tacos so much easier. The consistency and texture of the finished taco filling is much like pulled pork, and again no one died, there is no saturated fat, no cholesterol and it is scrumptious!

Eat Your Vegetables, Bitches

2 20- ounce cans Jackfruit in water or brine
   (Not in syrup!)
1-2 TBLS olive oil
1 medium yellow onion, chopped
4-5 cloves garlic, chopped
1 1/2 TBLS chili powder
1 1/2 TBLS ground cumin
1 TBLS smoked paprika

1/2 - 1 small chipotle pepper in adobo sauce, chopped,
   *WARNING! These peppers are spicy, so start with
   less and add. Same with the adobo sauce.
1 tsp adobo sauce, more if you like spice!
3 TBLS Bragg's Liquid Aminos or coconut aminos
2/3 cup vegetable broth
3 TBLS lime juice

12 Corn tortillas
4 cups shredded cabbage
Chopped cilantro
Chopped onions

Diced tomatoes
Lime wedges
Salsa
Or make Spicy Cabbage Slaw *(Salads and Whatnot)*

Drain and rinse the Jackfruit. Sort through the pieces and cut off the center core if it is hard. Use your hands to pull and shred the Jackfruit. Rinse again and drain well in a colander. Dry thoroughly.

In a large skillet, heat 1 TBLS olive oil over medium high and add the onions. Sauté for 4-5 minutes or until the onions are beginning to be golden. Add the garlic and cook for another minute, stirring.

Add the Jackfruit, chili powder, cumin, paprika and stir well. Add the chipotle peppers and adobo sauce (start with 1/2 a pepper and taste for spice, you can always add more!), liquid aminos, vegetable broth and lime juice. Stir well, reduce heat to medium-low and cover. Cook for about 20 minutes, stirring several times. After the 20 minutes use two forks to continue pulling and shredding, for a "meat-like" texture. Taste and adjust the spices, if necessary. Add more paprika and or cumin if you like a smokey flavor. Add more chipotle pepper and/or adobo sauce for spicier tacos! Or liquid aminos or lime for a saltier flavor!

Turn the heat up to medium-high and cook for 2-3 more minutes. Remove from heat.

For Tacos:
If you have a gas stove, turn the flame on medium and place a corn tortilla on the burner. Using tongs turn the tortilla every 10 seconds or so…do not allow to burn. The tortillas will firm up and get a little crispy. This way they won't just fall apart! Keep them warm in the oven as you prepare the rest of the tortillas. Or, warm the tortillas in the microwave wrapped in paper towels.

Fill the tortillas with Jackfruit taco "meat", shredded cabbage, chopped tomatoes, chopped onions, sliced avocado and salsa. Spicy Cabbage Slaw is a great way to go! Or, however you dig your tacos! Serve with wedges of lime!

• A squeeze of Karam's Garlic Sauce is Da Bomb!

• You can serve these as Lettuce Wraps, as well! Use Romaine or Butter lettuce leaves.

• You can store leftovers Jackfruit Taco "meat" in the refrigerator for 4-5 days, or in the freezer for 1 month!

Eat Your Vegetables, Bitches

Spanakopita

Serves 4 as an entrée

Here is another favorite I thought I would have to give up when I became Plant Based. But, with my Vegan Goat Cheese recipe we can have Spanakopita and eat it, too! You can make this recipe with 2 pounds of fresh spinach or simplify your life and use frozen spinach. Frozen is the next best thing to fresh, because vegetables are picked at the peak of ripeness, blanched and quickly frozen, which retains nutrients. So, don't hesitate to use frozen spinach in this awesome recipe!

1- 1 lb. package phyllo pastry, defrosted at
    room temperature and kept covered
1/2 cup Earth Balance, melted
2 lbs. fresh spinach or 16 ounces of frozen spinach
    (thawed and water squeezed out)

1 TBLS olive oil
1 large onion, finely chopped
3 TBLS fresh dill, chopped or 2 TBLS dried dill
Salt and pepper
1 recipe Vegan Goat Cheese *(Hors d'Oeuvres)*

Preheat oven to 375 degrees. Unfold the Phyllo on a flat surface. Cover with a clean towel. Make sure the Phyllo is cut to the size of your baking dish. A 9 x 13 inch baking dish is perfect!

If you are using fresh spinach, take the stems off, wash and dry the leaves and coarsely chop the leaves with a sharp knife.

Heat the olive oil in a large sauté pan over medium high and cook the chopped onions until they are soft. Add the fresh or frozen spinach and stir well over medium heat for about 5 minutes. Turn the heat up for a minute to help evaporate excess moisture. Remove from heat and allow to cool. When this is cool, mix in the dill, vegan goat cheese, salt and pepper.

Spray the bottom and sides of the baking dish. Melt the Earth Balance. Lay one sheet of Phyllo in the bottom of the baking dish, then brush lightly with the melted Earth Balance. Repeat this step for six layers.

Spread the filling evenly over the Phyllo and top with six or seven more layers of Phyllo, brushing each layer with Earth Balance.

Sprinkle with a little water and bake for 40 minutes, until golden. Allow to stand for 10 minutes before cutting.

Serve with Greek Salad in the Round *(Salads and Whatnot)* and Rice Pilaf *(On the Side)*.

 Dolmades

(Stuffed Grape Leaves)
Makes about 40

The first time I had Greek food was when I was eighteen years old, and my boyfriend, George Callins took me to Demo's in San Antonio, Texas. The flavors were so unusual to me, and I must admit it took a few times before I said, "Hey George, let's go get Greek food." But once I crossed that line with my taste buds there was no going back! George's family is Greek on both sides, so I got to experience a lot of Greek food…and Retsina, at that time in my life. When George and I moved to Los Angeles, he would get his Mom on the phone to describe how to make different Greek dishes. I learned a lot about food with George, and it was he who awakened the Foodie in me! Thanks George! I muddled through making the recipes his Mom described and the food was always delicious. I have veganized my recipe of Dolmades and they are scrumptious!

1 medium onion, finely chopped
1 package Trader Joe's Beefless Ground Beef
1 1/2 cups cooked long grain rice
    (measure the cooked rice)
2 TBLS chopped fresh mint
2 TBLS chopped fresh dill OR 1 TBLS dry

2 TBLS chopped fresh parsley
1/3 cup pine nuts
1 1/2 tsp granulated garlic
1 jar 8-9 ounces Grape Leaves
1/4 cup olive oil +1 TBLS
Juice of 1 lemon

Drain the grape leaves and set aside. Heat 1 TBLS olive oil in a sauté pan and cook the onion over medium high heat until soft. Add the Beefless Ground Beef and stir. Add the rice, mint, dill, parsley, pine nuts and granulated garlic. Stir well. Taste and add salt, if necessary.

Spread the grape leaves out on a flat surface, vein side up one at a time. Add a heaping spoonful of filling near the stem end. Fold the sides of the leaves over the filling then roll up tightly. Place the Dolmades seam side down in a large pot. Mix the lemon juice and olive oil and pour over the Dolmades. Add about 1 cup of Hot water, just enough to come about halfway up the sides of the Dolmades. Place a plate on top of the Dolmades to hold them in place. Put the lid on the pot and cook gently over medium to medium low heat for about 40 minutes. DO NOT ALLOW THE WATER TO TOTALLY EVAPORATE AND BURN. **Check on them while cooking!**

Remove the Dolmades to a plate and garnish with lemon wedges.

Serve with Tzatziki *(Sauces and Such).*

These are great as hors d'oeuvres, as well!

Grilled Tofu with Red Onion Marmalade

Serves 2

This Tofu recipe is super flavorful and, Red Onion Marmalade…need I say more?

1 Box organic Firm Tofu, well drained

Marinade

1 TBLS Sesame Oil	1/2 cup orange juice
5 TBLS Bragg's Liquid Aminos or soy or tamari sauce	1/4 cup warm water
3 cloves garlic, pressed	Olive oil or Canola spray
1 TBLS Miso	1 tsp olive oil

Drain the tofu well and press between several layers of paper towels. Change the paper towels and place a plate on top of the paper towel wrapped tofu and allow to sit for 10 minutes. Meanwhile, combine the marinade ingredients and whisk well. Set the tofu flat on a cutting board, long side facing you, and slice into rectangles 1/2 inch thick. Place the tofu in a large Ziplock and pour the marinade over. Zip it tight and gently arrange the tofu flat in the bag. Refrigerate for at least 1 hour, longer if possible. Flip the bag halfway through the marinating time.

While the tofu is marinating you can make the Red Onion Marmalade.

Red Onion Marmalade

2 medium red onions	2 TBLS balsamic vinegar
1 TBLS olive oil	Salt and pepper

Thinly slice the red onions and toss in a bowl with the Balsamic, salt and pepper. Mix well. Heat 1 TBLS of olive oil in a large sauté pan over medium-high heat. Add the red onion mixture and lower the heat to medium-low. Cook stirring often until the onions are very soft, about 15 minutes. Do not let them brown.

After 1 or more hours of marinating, spray a cast iron skillet or heavy skillet and add a tsp of olive oil. Heat over high until very hot but not smoking.

Add the tofu (not the marinade) and reduce the heat to medium high. Keep the tofu moving in the pan. Allow to cook for 3-4 minutes then check to see if it is browning. You want a nice medium brown color. Turn the tofu and cook on the other side. When brown on both sides, pour some of the marinade over the tofu and allow the marinade to reduce. Arrange the tofu on plates and top with a nest of the red onion marmalade.

Serve immediately with rice or quinoa and a green salad!

Asian Tofu

2 Servings

This tofu is versatile and can be used in a variety of recipes.
The longer you allow the tofu to sit in the marinade, the more flavorful it will be.

1 box organic firm or extra firm tofu, drained on paper towels
1 tsp olive oil
2 TBLS toasted sesame oil
3 TBLS Tamari, Soy or Bragg's Liquid Aminos
3 cloves garlic, pressed
2 tsp fresh ginger, finely chopped or 1 tsp ginger powder
A pinch – 1/2 teaspoon crushed red pepper or
1 tsp Siracha Sauce (optional) more if you like it spicy!
3 TBLS orange juice
1 TBLS rice vinegar

Pour the water off the tofu and wrap in paper towels to drain. Slice into 1/2 inch thick pieces and put on paper towels to drain, about 5 minutes.

In a large skillet add olive oil, sesame oil, Bragg's or Tamari sauce, garlic, ginger, crushed red pepper, orange juice and rice vinegar. Bring to a gentle boil over medium high heat then add the tofu. Cook over medium high heat for about 2 minutes, turn the tofu over and cook for 2 more minutes. Cover and reduce heat to low and allow the tofu to cook for about 5 minutes. Turn the tofu over and cover again for about 5 minutes. You can leave it in longer for a crispy texture, allowing the marinade to evaporate.

Serve with brown rice or Yellow Coconut Rice *(On the Side)* and vegetables or Asian Tofu Bowl *(Salads and Whatnot).*

Pasta Caprese

Serves 4

I first created this dish on a summer day when I had an abundance of tomatoes on hand. It is so fresh and light, yet can be made on a winter evening served with crusty Italian bread. If you don't have fresh tomatoes, don't fret. Just use canned diced tomatoes and call it good!

1 TBLS olive oil
1 medium yellow onion, chopped
3 cloves garlic, chopped
1/4 tsp red pepper flakes (or more, if you like spice!)
1 TBLS Italian herbs
4 cups fresh tomatoes, diced with juice or 2 – 14 oz.
    cans diced tomatoes
    (I prefer San Marzano canned tomatoes)

1/2 cup dry white wine
Salt and pepper
1/2 cup fresh vegan mozzarella, finely cubed
    (May I suggest Miyoko's Creamery Fresh
    Vegan Mozzarella. It's quite authentic!)
12 large fresh basil leaves, rolled and sliced
1 package fusilli or penne pasta

In a large sauté pan heat the olive oil over medium high heat. Add the onions and allow to cook for 3 minutes, stirring. Add in the garlic, red pepper flakes and Italian herbs, stir and cook for 1 minute.

Add the tomatoes, wine, salt and pepper and stir. Reduce the heat to medium low and cover. Simmer for 15 minutes, stirring twice.

Meanwhile, cook the pasta according to package instructions. Drain and return to the pot. While the pasta is cooking, stack the basil leaves on top of each other, roll up from the stem to the tip and cut the roll to create ribbons. Add half of the basil ribbons to the sauce and stir. Pour the tomato sauce over the pasta and toss to fully combine. Turn the pasta out into a large shallow bowl. Scatter the vegan mozzarella over the pasta. Scatter the remaining basil ribbons on top.

Eat Your Vegetables, Bitches

CauliFalafel

Makes about 16 small Falafel and serves 4

Okay…What? That's right, Falafel made with Cauliflower! Super tasty, super nutritious!
I have Veganized and changed a bit, a recipe that my friends Kim and Joe Illig shared.
"Be brrrrave Little Piglet", and try it! This recipe calls for Egg Replacer.
You can buy Ener G Egg Replacer, or you can make a flax egg by combining
1 TBLS flaxseed meal and 2.5 TBLS water. This makes one egg. Easy Peasy!
And these are great Hors d'Oeuvres, too! Just make them into CauliFalafel Bites!

Falafel

3 packed cups Cauliflower Rice
3/4 cup slivered almonds, coarsely ground or pounded
1 heaping TBLS cumin
1 flat TBLS coriander
1 tsp salt
1/2 tsp cayenne pepper

2 cloves garlic, pressed
2 TBLS fresh parsley, chopped
Egg Replacer for 3 eggs
4 TBLS all-purpose, almond or coconut flour

Canola Oil or your favorite lite vegetable oil

Tahini Sauce

4 TBLS tahini paste
4 TBLS warm water
4 TBLS lemon juice

2 garlic cloves, pressed
1/4 tsp salt to taste

Using a food processor with the shredding blade, process enough Cauliflower to make 3 cups. Or, Costco sells Organic Cauliflower Rice, in the freezer section.

Grind or pound the slivered almonds until they are ground but still a bit chunky for texture. Combine all the ingredients through flour and stir well, adding a little water if the mixture to too dry and not sticking together. Refrigerate while you make the tahini sauce.

For the tahini sauce, combine all the ingredients and stir well until smooth. Refrigerate.

Heat just enough vegetable oil to cover the bottom of a frying pan. You don't want them swimming in oil. Heat the oil until hot but not smoking. Turn the heat down to medium high.

While the oil is heating, with wet hands start forming the falafel into 3 inch disks that are about 1/2 inch thick. Gently put them in the pan 5 or 6 at a time, so they are not crowded. When they start turning brown around the edges lift one to see if it is brown, then turn. Don't turn too soon! We want them nicely browned! Place the cooked falafel on a plate lined with a couple of layers of paper towels to drain.

Serve with pita, sliced tomatoes, kalamata olives and the tahini sauce!

Shepherd's Pie Portobellos

Serves 4

This is a wonderful and hearty dish that can be served as a Holiday dinner, or just on a Thursday! It is yummy and soul warming.

---

6 medium potatoes
3-4 TBLS Earth Balance
1/3 – 2/3 cups milk like substance, plain, unflavored
        (almond, rice, soy, oat) or vegetable broth
Fresh ground Black Pepper and a little salt
4 large Portobello mushrooms, cleaned and stems saved
2 zucchinis, chopped
1 medium onion, chopped

3-4 garlic cloves, pressed
2 carrots, peeled and diced
1 cup peas, fresh or frozen
2 TBLS olive oil
3 TBLS balsamic vinegar
1/2 cup vegan sharp cheddar cheese,
        grated (optional)
Granulated garlic

Peel the potatoes and cut into big chunks. Put the potatoes into a pot of water and turn on high heat. When the water starts to boil turn the heat down to medium and allow to cook for about 10-12 minutes…until the potatoes are fork tender. Drain (but save 1/3 cup of potato water) and put into the mixer. Add the Earth Balance, salt and pepper and a little of the milk or broth. Mix on medium and add more milk as you mix. Add milk slowly! The mashed potatoes should be thick and creamy. Keep warm.

While the potatoes are cooking, prepare the mushrooms by cleaning them with a damp paper towel. Remove the stems and set them aside. Scrape out the underside of the mushrooms (gills).

Meanwhile, back on the ranch…Chop the mushroom stems, onion and zucchini and dice the carrots. Heat 1 TBLS olive oil in a large sauté pan and add the vegetables. Cook for 3 minutes. Add the garlic, peas, salt and pepper to taste. Reduce the heat to medium, stir and cook for about 5-6 minutes, until veggies begin to soften. Stir in the vegan cheese and allow to melt.

Preheat the oven to 375 degrees.

Put 1 TBLS of olive oil in a large sauté pan and heat over medium high heat. Add 1 TBLS of balsamic vinegar and the Portobello mushrooms, top side down. Add the rest of the balsamic onto the mushrooms, sprinkle with granulated garlic, salt and pepper on the underside and move them around to coat. Reduce heat to medium-low. Cook about 6-8 minutes, turning once.

Place the portobellos on a sprayed cookie sheet and heap in the veggies then cover with mashed potatoes. Be generous! Pile them high! Bake for about 15 minutes. You can deglaze the mushroom pan with the saved potato water. Add a little at a time and allow to reduce (get thickish) and drizzle the balsamic glaze on top when the mushrooms come out of the oven.

Eat Your Vegetables, Bitches

Simple Red and Green Curry

Serves 2 as a main course

Mixing red and green curry…what? Yes!
It's a flavor sensation, and not against the proverbial curry rules.
Depending on how spicy your curry paste is, you may want to omit the crushed red pepper.

1 TBLS olive oil
1 medium onion, diced
1 large zucchini, large dice or ½ inch rounds, about 2 cups
1 medium carrot, peeled and sliced
3-4 cloves garlic, chopped
1/8 – 1 tsp crushed red pepper

1 heaping TBLS red curry paste
1 heaping TBLS green curry paste
1 tsp turmeric
1 cup vegetable broth
2 cups of cooked lentils or chickpeas
1 cup coconut milk

Heat the olive oil in a sauté pan over medium high heat. Add the onion, reduce heat to medium and cook stirring for 3 minutes. Add the zucchini and carrots and cook for 3 minutes. Add the garlic, crushed red pepper, red and green curry paste, turmeric, vegetable broth, and stir for 1 minute. Add the lentils or chickpeas. Stir well, reduce heat to medium low and cover. Simmer for 10 minutes or until carrots are done. Add 1 cup of Coconut Milk, and heat through.

Serve over Yellow Coconut Rice *(On the Side)*!

Spicy Tofu

Serves 2

This delicious tofu goes amazingly well with Stir- Fry, in Veggie Pad Thai, over rice or on the side of Asian Angel Hair. It comes together in just a few minutes!

1 box firm or extra firm tofu, drained
Olive oil or canola spray
2 tsp sesame oil
1 tsp olive oil

1 – 2 TBLS Sriracha
1 – 2 TBLS Bragg's Liquid Aminos or
    Soy Sauce
1 – 2 TBLS Hoisin Sauce

Cut the drained tofu into one inch cubes. Spray the wok or sauté pan, add the sesame and olive oil and heat over high heat. Toss in the tofu, reduce heat to medium high and allow to cook untouched for about three minutes. Shake the wok or pan and flip individual pieces to brown on other sides. Allow to cook for another two minutes. Shake the wok again. Turn on the fan (trust me!) and add the Sriracha, Bragg's and Hoisin and gently stir well to coat. Allow to cook for another minute or two. Shake the wok to keep the tofu moving. Turn out into a pretty bowl or add to a variety of dishes.

Thai Basil Eggplant

Serves 2 - 4

I love the way spices and fresh herbs interweave and create taste sensations.
Thai dishes are always an adventure for the taste buds. The fresh basil in this dish and as a finishing touch on top is la pièce de résistance. I do not know how to express this in Thai, but your mouth will translate!

2 TBLS olive oil
1 large Italian eggplant, unpeeled, diced
1 medium yellow onion, sliced
1 large red bell pepper, sliced
2 cups mushrooms, sliced

5 cloves garlic, pressed
1 tsp fresh ginger, minced
1/2 cup fresh basil leaves, coarsely chopped
2-3 TBLS fresh basil, leaves rolled and
    sliced into ribbons

Sauce
2 TBLS Bragg's Liquid Aminos or
    Tamari sauce or Soy sauce
1/3 cup vegetable broth
4 TBLS Hoisin sauce
2 tsp corn starch

1 TBLS chili sauce (or more for a spicier dish!)
1 TBLS Lemongrass puree or paste
1-2 TBLS maple syrup, depending on
    how much sweet you like

Dice the unpeeled eggplant into 1 inch cubes. Heat 1 TBLS olive oil in a large sauté pan over medium high heat. Add the eggplant and stir. Add 3 TBLS vegetable broth, stir and cover. Reduce heat to medium low and cook for 8 minutes. Stir every couple of minutes, adding a bit more broth if the eggplant sticks to the pan. Not too much broth, or the eggplant will get mushy. Remove from heat. Take the lid off.

Meanwhile, cut the onion in half and slice lengthwise in 1/4 inch strips. Cut the red pepper in half and remove the seeds and core. Cut each half in half then into 1/2 inch strips. In a separate sauté pan heat 1 TBLS olive oil over medium high heat then add the onions and red bell pepper. Cook for 2 minutes, stir, then add the mushrooms. Cook for another minute and add the garlic and ginger. Stir well and allow to cook for 2-3 minutes. You want the onions and veggies cooked, but firm. Remove from heat.

Make the sauce by combining all the ingredients in order. Whisk well until the cornstarch is well combined. Pour the onions, peppers and mushrooms over the eggplant and heat on medium high, stirring. When the vegetables are hot add the sauce and stir. Cook for about 2 minutes on medium high until the sauce has thickened. Turn off the heat and add the 1/2 cup of chopped basil and stir to combine. Just before serving top with the sliced basil ribbons.

Serve over brown rice, quinoa or Yellow Coconut Rice *(On the Side)*.

On the Side

Eat Your Vegetables, Bitches

On the Side

Eat Your Vegetables, Bitches

Vegan Cheesy Polenta

Serves 4 - 6

This is a recipe from my friend Jeffrey Lemkin on Camano Island. I met Jeffrey at the Women's Expo when I lived on the Island. Jeffrey was sampling his polenta, and let me tell you, it was delish! I have veganized his recipe, and it is still delish! The instructions below are pretty much Jeffrey's, word for word that he sent in a Messenger text.

Thanks Jeffrey!

---

4 1/2 cups vegetable broth
4 TBLS Earth Balance
1 tsp salt or to taste
1 cup polenta

6 ounces vegan sharp cheddar
4 ounces vegan cream cheese, cut into several pieces.
1/2 tsp or to taste – chipotle powder or cayenne pepper
1/2 tsp fresh ground black pepper

Optional: A handful of finely chopped fresh green herbs –
thyme, rosemary, chives, parsley, tarragon – Any of these herbs will be delicious!

Preheat the oven to 350 degrees.

Put the vegetable broth, Earth Balance and salt in a big pot. Bring to a boil. Slooooowly add the polenta, stirring constantly with a wooden spoon. Reduce heat to a low bubbling simmer and keep stirring.

Stir, scraping the bottom with your spoon, to keep the polenta from sticking and burning. Do this contemplative stirring ritual for perhaps 10-12 minutes. The polenta should be getting pretty thick. When you decide the polenta is "pretty thick", add the cheeses, the chipotle or cayenne, and the black pepper. Stir, stir, stir, until the cheese has totally been absorbed by the polenta. Remove from stovetop, add the (optional) fresh herbs now and stir in.

Whole Lotta stirring going on, but it's worth it!

With a rack in the middle of the preheated oven, spray a 9x13 inch baking dish – scrape out the polenta into the dish, and top with a little more of the finely chopped herbs, if you choose to use herbs. Pop the dish into oven and bake for 25 minutes or until quite firm and just starting to brown a bit on the top. Remove from oven, let it cool for a bit. The polenta will set as it cools. You can serve it hot, warm, or cold.

It is great with a dollop of Basil Pesto *(Sauces and Such)*, served with Ratatouille or Roasted Vegetables *(Green Things, Yellow Things…)*.

Roasted Fingerling Potatoes and Brussels Sprouts

Serves 4

Another delicious way to cook these nutrient packed morsels,
with the added twist of the darling of the potato family:
The Fingerling!

---

1 pound brussels sprouts, washed, stemmed and halved
1 1/2 pounds fingerling potatoes,
      scrubbed and cut in half lengthwise
1 large shallot, finely diced

3 cloves garlic, finely chopped
1 heaping TBLS fresh rosemary, finely chopped
2 TBLS olive oil
A little salt and freshly ground pepper

Preheat the oven to 400 degrees. Spray a large rimmed baking sheet with olive oil or canola spray.

Put the brussels sprouts, fingerling potatoes, shallots, garlic, rosemary and olive oil in a large bowl. Stir well to coat. Transfer to the baking sheet in one layer and sprinkle with salt and pepper.

Bake for 25-35 minutes, stirring them up with a spatula halfway through.

Garnish with a sprig of rosemary.

CauliFlower Rice

Makes about 6 servings

The Powerhouse of Nutrition!

---

1 head cauliflower, cut into florets and finely "riced"
1 TBLS olive oil
3/4 cup finely chopped onion

2 cloves garlic, pressed
1/3 cup vegetable broth

In your food processor, using the grating or shredding attachment, process the cauliflower florets. If you do not have a food processor, simply grate the cauliflower with a cheese grater or use a chopper.

Heat the oil in a large sauté pan, skillet or wok over medium-high heat. Lower heat to medium, add the onion and cook, stirring for about 3-4 minutes. DO NOT BROWN. Toss in the garlic and cook for 1 minute.

Add the "riced" cauliflower and cook for about 5-6 minutes, stirring often.

Add 1/3 cup of vegetable broth and cover to steam for 5 minutes on low heat, stirring once, until the cauliflower is cooked through and the broth has absorbed. Raise the heat at the end of the cooking time if there is still liquid in the pan.

Serve with any dish as a replacement for rice!

Mashed CauliFlower

Serves 4

Who doesn't love mashed potatoes…I mean Cauliflower!

---

1 medium head cauliflower, cut into florets
1 tsp granulated garlic
3 TBLS Earth Balance
1/4 cup of unsweetened and unflavored almond milk or Vegetable Broth
A little salt and freshly ground pepper
Vegan cheddar or pepper jack, if you like.

Place a steamer basket in a pot with a couple of inches of water and bring to a boil. Place the cauli-flower florets in the steamer basket, cover and steam for 15 minutes, or until the cauliflower is very tender. Drain the water and put the cauliflower in the food processor, mixer or old school in a bowl with a hand masher. Sprinkle on the granulated garlic, add the Earth Balance, almond milk or broth, salt and pepper. Process until you have a smooth, lump free consistency. Top with some vegan ched-dar or pepper jack, if that tickles your fancy!

Mashed Potatoes

Serves 4

My son, Jack makes the Best Mashed Potatoes. The young man has a knack for just the right combination of butter-like substance, almond milk, salt and pepper. They are perfect every time he makes them! May your Mashed Potatoes be as delicious as the ones on our table!

8 medium russet potatoes, peeled and cut into 2 inch chunks	1/4 cup vegetable broth
4 TBLS Earth Balance	1 tsp granulated garlic
1/3+ cup almond, hemp or oat milk or soy creamer (unsweetened and unflavored)	1 tsp salt and 1/2 tsp pepper

Wash, peel and cut the potatoes into 2 inch chunks and put into a big pot of cold water. Turn the heat on high and bring to a boil. Reduce heat to medium and cook for about 20 minutes or until the potatoes are soft, but not falling apart. Drain the potatoes (save the potato water for soup!) and put into a Cuisinart or a mixing bowl with the Earth Balance, almond milk, broth, granulated garlic, salt and pepper. Beat on medium speed, adding more liquid if the potatoes are too stiff. Keep warm until served!

Garlic & Chive Mashed Parsnips with Potatoes

Serves 4

Parsnips are a highly nutritious root vegetable, full of fiber and antioxidants!
A nice twist on traditional mashed potatoes. And, another opportunity to add in more nutrition!
The parsnips give this dish a slightly sweet taste.

1 lb. parsnips, scrubbed and sliced 1 inch thick	1/4 cup (or more) Earth Balance
1 1/2 lbs. Yukon gold or russet potatoes, peeled and cut into 2" chunks	1/4 cup fresh chives, finely chopped
5-6 cloves garlic, finely chopped	Salt and pepper

Bring a large pot of water to a boil.

Add the potatoes and parsnips, reduce heat to medium. Allow to cook for about 16-18 minutes. They should be very tender, but not falling apart.

Gently drain into a colander. (save at least 1cup of the liquid for mixing)

Add the Earth Balance and garlic to a small pan over medium low heat. Keep the garlic moving in the pan for about 1-2 minutes. DO NOT allow the garlic to brown! Remove from heat. Toss in the chopped chives.

Put everything into a mixer or bowl for mashing. Mix or mash adding a bit of the cooking liquid a little at a time until thick, smooth and creamy. Taste and add salt and pepper, if you like.

Asian Angel Hair

Serves 4

This is one of my daughter, Chrissie's favorite Go-To meals!

---

1 16 ounce package angel hair pasta, cooked al dente or your favorite
     Gluten Free Pasta cooked by package instructions
2 TBLS olive oil
4 TBLS toasted sesame oil
4-5 TBLS Tamari, Soy Sauce or Bragg's Liquid Aminos
3-4 cloves garlic, pressed
1 cup red bell pepper, finely diced or green bell pepper, or both!
1/4 to 1/2 teaspoon cayenne pepper
2 cups fresh spinach, finely chopped

Bring a big pot of water to a boil, Cook angel hair pasta for about 3 minutes, or a bit less than the package instructions. Or cook Gluten Free pasta to package instructions. Drain well and run under cold water to stop the cooking.

To a large sauté pan add the olive oil, sesame oil, soy sauce, garlic, red bell pepper and cayenne. Sauté over medium-high heat for one minute. Turn off heat. Add the pasta and spinach and toss well.

Serve with Asian Tofu or with Stir-fry or as Chrissie likes it…in a big bowl on its own with chopsticks!

Rice Pilaf

Serves 4

I remember the first time I had rice pilaf. I thought I had died and gone to heaven!
I just love the textures of rice mingling with orzo! Rice Pilaf is SO not boring!

---

1 TBLS Earth Balance
1 TBLS olive oil
1 small onion, finely chopped
1 tsp turmeric
1/2 cup Orzo pasta

2 cloves garlic, minced
1 cup long grain white rice, rinsed
2 TBLS fresh parsley, chopped
1 tsp salt
2 cups vegetable broth

In a large sauté pan heat the Earth Balance and olive oil over medium high heat. Add the onion, turmeric and orzo, stir and reduce heat to medium, cooking for about 3-4 minutes. Add the garlic and cook for another minute. Add the rice, 1 TBLS parsley, salt, vegetable broth and stir to combine. Bring to a boil then reduce heat to medium low and cover. Simmer for 18 minutes then remove from heat and allow to stand covered for 5 minutes.

Fluff with a fork, sprinkle a bit more chopped parsley and serve with Baked Greek Veggies *(Green Things, Yellow Things…)*, Cabbage Rolls, Dolmades *(Main Courses)* or whatever sparks your taste buds.

Garlic Baked Fries

Serves 3 - 4

So yummy served with Portobello Mushroom Burgers or Carrot Dogs,
with Garlic Aioli on the side!

---

4 large russet potatoes, scrubbed and cut into
    long wedges (leave the skin on)
2 TBLS of olive oil
1 tsp salt

1 tsp oregano
1 tsp basil
2 tsp granulated garlic
2 tsp paprika

Preheat the oven to 400 degrees.

Wash and scrub the potatoes and cut into long wedges. Put them into a big bowl, add the olive oil and toss to coat well. In a small bowl mix together the salt, herbs, granulated garlic and paprika. Sprinkle on the potatoes and toss well to coat.

Put the potato wedges on a foil covered cookie sheet and bake for 40 minutes at 400 degrees. Turn halfway through cooking to brown on both sides. Serve with garlic aioli and/or ketchup!

Spanish Rice

Serves 4

A plate of Mexican food is not complete without Spanish Rice.

---

1 1/2 cups jasmine rice, rinsed
1 TBLS olive oil
1 medium yellow or white onion, diced
2 cloves garlic, chopped
1 TBLS cumin
1 TBLS oregano

1 tsp paprika
1-14 ounce can diced tomatoes
1 TBLS tomato paste
1 1/2 cups vegetable broth
2 tsp salt
1 tsp pepper

In a large sauté pan heat the olive oil and add the rice and onions. Cook over medium high heat stirring for about 3-4 minutes, until the rice begins to turn golden. Add the garlic and stir for 1 minute. Add the rest of the ingredients and stir well. Bring to a boil, reduce heat to low, cover and simmer for 20 minutes. Taste and adjust the seasonings, if necessary. Fluff with a fork before serving.

Serve with Jackfruit Tacos, CauliWally Tacos, Veggie Fajitas *(Main Courses)* or a side of beans and tortillas with guacamole and salsa!

Yellow Coconut Rice

Serves 6

Not only is this rice yummy, but it is beautiful! The rich golden color from turmeric brightens whatever you are serving with this lovely rice!

Rice Cooker Version:

Using the measuring cup that come with your rice cooker:
3 cups sticky rice or basmati rice, rinsed
2 tsp turmeric

1 - 14 oz. can coconut milk,
full fat or reduced fat
Water

Spray the bottom of your rice cooker. Rinse the rice well with cold water in a strainer. Put the rinsed rice in the rice cooker, add the turmeric and coconut milk, stir. Add water up to the 3 line in your rice cooker and push ON! It's that simple!

Stove top:

2 cups sticky rice or basmati rice, rinsed
2 tsp turmeric

1-14 oz can coconut milk
2 1/4 cups water

Rinse the rice well with cold water in a strainer. Put the rice, turmeric, coconut milk and water in a pot over high heat and stir to combine. Bring to a boil then reduce heat to low, stir and cover. Allow to cook undisturbed for 20 minutes. Remove from heat and allow to sit for 5 minutes. Fluff with a fork before serving.

Serve with Indian Lentil Curry, Thai Basil Eggplant, Roasted Pepper Curry with Spinach, Potatoes, and Mushrooms *(Main Courses)*.

Beans, Beans!

Eat Your Vegetables, Bitches

Beans, Beans!

You can take the girl out of Texas, but you can't take Texas out of the girl! Sometimes my Southern roots get the better of me, and I just gotta have some beans and cornbread!
The good news is, beans are so good for us! They are an excellent
source of fiber and they have lots of protein.
But, don't get any crazy ideas that you have to "combine" beans with rice or
another carb in order to make a "perfect protein". Forget that! Just eat beans!
Beans, Beans, are good for your heart, the more you eat…You know the rest!
And speaking of that rhyme…

There are a couple of things to know about cooking beans. First, you need to soak them, otherwise you will get the farts! Soaking beans before you cook them helps to remove some of the indigestible sugars that cause them to be nicknamed, "The Musical Fruit"!
You can achieve the deflatulization process two ways:

1. Sort and rinse the beans then put them in a pot and cover the beans with at least three inches of cold water, and add 2 tsp of salt. Cover the pot and allow to sit overnight or at least eight hours. In the morning drain and rinse the beans and they are ready to cook!

2. If you don't have time to soak you can sort and rinse the beans, put them in a pot and cover with at least three inches of cold water and 2 tsp salt. Put the pot on the stove over high heat and bring to a boil. Stir, turn off the heat and cover the pot. Allow to sit for one hour. After one hour drain and rinse the beans and they are ready to cook!

Pot O' Pinto Beans   *150*

Lentils   *150*

Black Beans   *151*

Black Eyed Peas, Y'all!   *153*

Pot O'Pinto Beans

Makes about 6 cups

Beans are so easy to cook, and they freeze well, so I always make a big pot and
have some in the freezer for the next time I get the hankerin'!
One pound of beans makes about 6 cups of cooked beans.

---

1 pound dry pinto beans, sorted, rinsed and soaked
1 large yellow onion, diced
3 cloves garlic, chopped
1 - 14 oz. can diced tomatoes
2 TBLS cumin
1 tsp dried oregano

1 sliced or whole jalapeno (optional)
    (If sliced, remove the seeds!)
Vegetable broth or water to cover 3 inches
    over the beans in the pot
2 tsp salt and 1/2 tsp pepper

Sort, rinse and soak the beans. (Soaking directions above).   Put everything into a big pot, except the salt. Bring to a boil over high heat, then reduce the heat to low and cover. Cook the beans for about 2 hours, stirring every half hour and making sure they are covered with water. Add more broth or water, if necessary. When the beans are soft add 2 tsp of salt and stir well. Allow the beans to sit for 15 minutes before serving. Taste and adjust seasonings.

Lentils

Makes about 6 cups

Lentils are so great to have in the fridge! You can toss them in a salad, add them to Pomodoro Sauce for a "meaty" texture, combine them with a scoop of quinoa and some salsa, put them in a bowl and top with chopped cucumber, red onion and tomatoes and a little Balsamic! YUM!
P.S. Lentils do not need to be soaked…just rinsed well.

---

1 - 16 ounce bag of brown lentils, sorted and rinsed
Olive oil or Canola spray
1 medium yellow onion, diced
1 medium carrot, peeled and diced
2 stalks celery, diced

3 cloves garlic, chopped
1 – 14 ounce can diced tomatoes with juice
1 bay leaf
Vegetable broth to cover 3 inches above the lentils
1 tsp each salt and pepper to taste

Sort and rinse the lentils. Spray a big pot and heat over medium high.   Reduce heat to medium and add the onions, carrots and celery. Cook stirring for about 4-5 minutes until the onions are becoming translucent. Add the garlic and stir for one minute. Add the lentils, tomatoes, bay leaf and broth and bring to a boil, stir well. Cover and reduce heat to low and simmer for about 40 minutes stirring occasionally, until the lentils are soft but whole. When the lentils are done add salt and pepper.

Black Beans

Makes about 6 cups

Black Beans are so versatile, you can use them for tostadas, chalupas, soups, tacos, burritos, salads, and so much more!
You definitely want to soak black beans, though…or maybe it's just me.
You can cook these babies with water, but why not kick up the flavor with vegetable broth?

1 – 1 pound bag Black Beans, sorted and soaked
1 medium yellow onion, chopped
Olive oil or canola oil spray
3 – 4 cloves garlic, chopped

2 bay leaves
8 cups vegetable broth
Salt and pepper to taste

Spray the bottom of a large stock pot and heat over medium high. Add the onions and sauté until becoming translucent, about 5 minutes. Add the garlic and cook stirring for 1 minute. Add the black beans, broth and bay leaves and bring to a boil. Reduce heat to low and simmer. Add more broth to keep the beans covered, if necessary. Check for doneness after 1 hour. Add salt and pepper to taste.

Black Eyed Peas, Y'all

Makes about 6 cups

'I've got a feelin'…that tonight's gonna be a good night…' WAIT! Not those Black Eyed Peas. Newsflash: Black Eyed Peas are not just to be eaten on New Year's Day for good luck. They are so delicious served alongside some sautéed greens with vinegar and a big hunk of cornbread! Yes, I'm from the South, but here's the secret…Black Eyed Peas are good for you! They contain so many nutrients, vitamins and minerals, they are a rich source of fiber, loaded with phytochemicals, they are high in lignans which may help prevent Osteoporosis, and they are a delicious source of plant based protein. And, they are so different from most legumes. All we are saying…is give Black Eyed Peas a chance.

---

1 – 1 pound bag of Black Eyed Peas, sorted, rinsed and soaked	1 jalapeno, seeds removed and finely chopped or 1/4-1/2 tsp cayenne pepper
Olive oil or canola oil spray	1 bay leaf
1 medium onion, diced	Vegetable broth to cover 2 inches
2 stalks celery, diced	Salt and pepper
1 carrot, peeled and diced	2 cups fresh spinach, coarsely chopped
3 cloves garlic, chopped	

Spray a big pot with olive oil spray and heat over medium high. Add the onions, celery and carrots and cook stirring for about 3 minutes. Add the garlic and jalapeno and cook for 1 minute stirring. Add the Black Eyed Peas, bay leaf and vegetable broth, stir.

Reduce heat to medium low, and cover with the lid tilted so steam can escape. Allow to cook for 1 hour, stirring once in a while. Test doneness after 45 minutes and add salt and pepper. Add the chopped spinach in the last 2 minutes of cooking.

Enjoy!

Sauces and Such...

Eat Your Vegetables, Bitches

Sauces and Such...

"It's all about the sauce." Where have I heard that before?
Sauces are a wonderful addition to so many dishes!
Ranging from Aioli to Tzatziki, a good sauce can make a meal great!

Basil Pesto

Makes one heaping cup

Pesto is very fun to make, especially in the summer when fresh basil is abundant.
Basil is easy to grow and so beautiful in the kitchen window!
Trader Joe's has amazingly healthy basil plants for about $4.

2 cups of packed basil leaves, washed,
    dried and stems removed
1/3 cup pine nuts
1/4 cup Nutritional Yeast

5 cloves garlic, coarsely chopped
1/4 cup Extra Virgin Olive Oil
1/2 tsp salt
1/2 tsp pepper

Place the basil, pine nuts, nutritional yeast and garlic in the food processor.
Pulse several times then scrape down the sides with a rubber spatula and pulse
several more times.

With the food processor running, slowly and steadily add the olive oil. Stop and scrape down the
sides of the food processor when necessary. Stir in salt and freshly ground pepper to taste.

Stir into hot pasta as soon as it is drained. Top with toasted pine nuts and a sprig of basil. A dollop
on top of Vegan "Cheesy" Polenta *(On the Side)* is something to write home about.

Tzatziki

Makes 1 1/2 cups

Tzatziki is a Mediterranean delight! It goes wonderfully with Dolmades, with Baked Greek Veggies, as a dip for vegetables and pita bread, as a salad dressing, or add a spoonful on top of Greek Salad or a baked potato! It is so fresh and cool in the summer!

---

8 ounces plain, unsweetened vegan yogurt
    (I really like the brand Kite Hill)
1/2 cup cucumber, peeled, seeded and finely chopped
1/4 cup red onion, finely diced

1-2 cloves garlic, pressed
1 TBLS dill
Juice of 1/2 a lemon (or more to taste!)
Salt and pepper

Peel the cucumber, cut in half and scrape out the seeds.

Finely chop 1/2 cup of the cucumber and squeeze the liquid out with a paper towel. Mix all the ingredients together, taste and adjust the seasonings.

Cover and refrigerate for at least one hour before serving, to allow the flavors to mingle.

Tahini Sauce

Makes about 1/2 cup

This is a great sauce for CauliFalafel or traditional Falafel. Delicious on salad or as a dip.

4 TBLS tahini paste
4 TBLS warm water
4 TBLS lemon juice

2 garlic clove, pressed
1/4 tsp salt, to taste

Combine all the ingredients and stir well until smooth.

Refrigerate.

You can easily double or triple the Tahini Sauce.

Vegan Ricotta

About 2 cups

In case you missed this recipe in Main Courses, it is worth repeating here because there are many things one can do with Vegan Ricotta besides Lasagna, Manicotti and Cannelloni. For instance you can add 1/2 - 1 cup to Pomodoro Sauce and create a magnificent creamy sauce for pasta, make a fresh and simple pasta with garlic, olive oil, lemon, crushed red pepper, chopped spinach and Vegan Ricotta, add into Mashed Potatoes for a little something extra, or as a pizza topping. Be creative!

2 cups raw cashews, soaked
2/3+ cup of water
3 cloves garlic, pressed
2 1/2 TBLS nutritional yeast

1 large lemon, juiced
1 tsp salt
1/2 tsp pepper

Soak the raw cashews in a bowl of cold water for 2 hours. If you do not have 2 hours to spare, you can boil a small pot of water, remove from heat, add the cashews and soak them for 30 minutes.

Drain the cashews and put all the ingredients into a food processor or blender. Process until the mixture resembles ricotta, scraping down the sides to keep it moving. It should be rather thick, smooth and creamy. Add additional water, if necessary, to keep the mixture moving in the blender or food processor.

This will keep in the refrigerator for 5-6 days.

Garlic Aioli

About 8 servings

This is simply delicious on everything from veggie burgers, fries, grilled tofu or vegetables.

1 cup vegan mayonnaise
5 medium sized cloves garlic, pressed
3 TBLS lemon juice (or more to taste)
1 tsp chili sauce like Sriracha (optional)
1/4 tsp salt
1/4 tsp pepper

Put everything into a bowl and whisk well. Cover and pop into the refrigerator for at least 30 minutes before serving. This stores well in the fridge!

Flax Eggs

Makes 1 Egg

Let's talk about eggs. There has been back and forth "information" on eggs for decades. One week they are good for you, the next they are bad. The studies that show eggs being good for you are sixty percent of the time conducted by…that's right, The Egg Industry!
The truth is, eggs are full of cholesterol. There is as much cholesterol in one egg as there is in an eight ounce steak. The yoke of an egg is meant to grow and nourish a baby chick in about 21 days.
And for me, more importantly is the way chickens are raised to produce eggs.
It is cruel and inhumane. Do a little research and see for yourself. Meanwhile, Flax Eggs are a great substitute for vegan cooking and baking. And bonus, flax is a Super Food!
Flax is high in nutrients, vitamins, minerals, protein, fiber and is anti-inflammatory.
Flax is great for your skin, heart, hormones and is a cancer fighter.
BOOM!

1 TBLS flax meal
2 1/2 TBLS water

Mix the flax meal and water in a small bowl and allow to sit for about 5 minutes in order to thicken. Double or triple this recipe for 2 or 3 eggs. Note: Flax eggs are not exactly like chicken eggs in some baking. But this recipe works well with the Vegan Ricotta in the Eggplant Lasagna recipe, and also most cookies, pancakes, muffins, cakes and lots of other recipes that call for eggs.

Chimichurri Sauce

About 1 cup

I used to make this sauce for steak, but it is scrumptious on grilled tofu and vegetables.
The herbs and spices co-mingle to create the most wonderful tang!

1/2 cup parsley, chopped	1 tsp granulated garlic
1/2 cup cilantro, chopped	1/2 tsp chili powder
4 cloves garlic, minced	1/2 tsp mustard powder
1 tsp oregano	1/4 tsp salt and 1/4 tsp pepper
1 tsp cumin	3 TBLS olive oil
1 tsp coriander	3 TBLS red wine vinegar
1 tsp onion granules	

Crush all the ingredients in a mortar or in a food processor until well combined and smooth. Use for grilled vegetables or tofu, mix in with caulirice or quinoa. Serve with crusty French or Italian bread.

"Creamy" Tomato Sauce

Serves 4

This delicious sauce comes together very quickly after the soaking of the cashews.

1/3 cup raw cashews, soaked	1/2 tsp salt
1 15 ounce can diced tomatoes	1/2 tsp pepper
2 heaping TBLS tomato paste	1/4-1/2 tsp crushed red pepper
3 garlic cloves, pressed	(optional, but delicious)
2 tsp Italian Herbs	1 tsp cumin
1 tsp onion powder	1 1/2 cups vegetable broth

Soak the raw cashews in cold water for at least 2 hours or if you do not have two hours, boil a pot of water, remove from heat and add the cashews. Soak for 30 minutes. Drain.

Into the blender goes the soaked cashews, diced tomatoes, tomato paste, garlic, Italian Herbs, onion powder, salt and pepper, crushed red pepper and cumin. Add the 1 1/2 cups of broth slowly as you blend well until creamy and smooth. Add more broth, depending on how thick you like your sauce.
*You can add 1/3 cup of Vodka to make this a Creamy Vodka Sauce.

Transfer to a pot, bring to a low boil, reduce heat and simmer on low for about 20 minutes.
Serve over pasta of your choice.

Eat Your Vegetables, Bitches

Mushroom Gravy Baby!

Makes about 4 cups

Who doesn't love gravy? Typically, gravy is made from the drippings (fatty grease)
of whatever meat you have cooked, often adding butter and/or cream.
Super high in saturated fats and, let's face it…Yummy!
This recipe calls for a small amount of plant based fat to take the flavors to that next level.

---

1 TBLS olive oil
1 TBLS Earth Balance
3 TBLS shallots, finely diced
2 cups mushrooms, sliced
1 clove garlic, pressed
1 1/2 tsp dried thyme
3/4 cup red wine
3 cups vegetable broth +3 TBLS
1 tsp Vegetable Better Than Bouillon
2 heaping TBLS flour or corn starch
Salt and pepper

In a large sauté pan melt the Earth Balance with the olive oil over medium high heat. Reduce the heat to medium, add the shallots and sauté for about 3 minutes. Add the mushrooms and stir well. Allow to cook for about 5 minutes, stirring halfway through, until they begin to brown and release their juices. Let them brown a bit!

Add the garlic and thyme and stir for 1 minute. Raise the heat to high and add the red wine. Allow this to reduce for 1 minute then add the vegetable broth and 1 tsp of Better Than Bouillon. Stir well. Bring to a boil then reduce the heat to medium, and simmer for 5 minutes.

Combine the flour or corn starch with the 3 TBLS vegetable broth and stir well so there are no lumps.

Add the flour mixture to the gravy and whisk well, breaking up any lumps.

Taste and add salt and pepper to your liking.

Serve over Mashed Potatoes, Mashed Cauliflower *(On the Side)* or with Shepherd's Pie Portobellos *(Main Courses)*.

Pomodoro Sauce

Serves 6

A good tomato sauce will go a long way in the recipe realm.
I always called tomato sauce Marinara from working in an Italian restaurant.
When I was in Italy at Abruzzo Cibus Cooking School, Massimo, the proprietario told us that in
Italian Marinara sauce means with seafood,
and that a simple tomato sauce would be called Pasta Al Pomodoro.
But it tastes like Italy, and that is all that matters!

---

2 TBLS olive oil
1 large onion, chopped
3 TBL minced garlic
1 TBLS dried oregano
1 TBLS dried basil
Or 2 TBLS dried Italian herbs
1/4 - 1 tsp crushed red pepper (optional)
1/2 cup dry red wine
2 – 28 ounce cans of diced tomatoes
2 TBLS tomato paste
1/2 tsp salt and 1/2 tsp freshly ground pepper
1/4-1/2 cup fresh basil, chopped

How chunky you like your Pomodoro sauce will determine how much of the tomatoes you will run through the blender. For a chunkier sauce, run 1/2 of the tomatoes through the blender. For a less chunky sauce, run 3/4 of the tomatoes through the blender. For no chunks, run all the tomatoes through the blender.

Heat the olive oil in a deep pot over medium high heat.

Add the chopped onions, reduce heat to medium and cook stirring until they become translucent, about 4-5 minutes. Add the garlic, dried herbs, crushed red pepper and sauté for 1 minute. Raise the heat to medium high, stir in the red wine and cook for 1 minute. Stir in the tomatoes, tomato paste, salt and pepper. Cover and cook on low for 30 minutes to 1 hour, stirring several times during cooking.

Stir in the fresh basil just before serving over your choice of pasta or in several recipes in this book. This is so delicious made the day before you serve!

Garnish with fresh chopped basil and basil leaves.

Garlic Olive Oil

Makes about 1 cup

This is a brilliant offering! So simple, versatile, and so delicious!
This olive oil takes up the garlic flavor and becomes magnificent!

1 cup Extra Virgin Olive Oil
5-8 cloves garlic, pressed

Combine the ingredients in a glass jar with a lid. Shake to combine.
Store in the refrigerator.

Use for sautéing vegetables, tofu dishes, salads or add fresh herbs, a little salt and crushed red pepper
and use as a dip for crusty Italian bread!

Spiced Cranberry Sauce

Makes about 3 cups

This is a beautiful and delicious accompaniment for Thanksgiving or Christmas.
This is a fairly tart recipe!

4 cups fresh whole cranberries,
    washed and picked over
1 cup water
1 cup orange juice
1 TBLS orange zest

1/2 tsp cinnamon
1/2 teaspoon nutmeg
1/4 teaspoon ground cloves
1/3 cup sugar
1 small can mandarin oranges, drained

In a large saucepan, combine the cranberries, water and orange juice and bring to a boil. Reduce heat
and simmer for 10 minutes, stirring often until skins have broken and the cranberries have broken
down.

Add in the orange zest, cinnamon, nutmeg, cloves, sugar and mandarin oranges. Simmer about 10
minutes until thick. The cranberry sauce will thicken more as it cools. Garnish with a sprig of your
favorite fresh herbs.

Serve on the side of Shepherd's Pie Portobellos *(Main Courses)* for a Holiday Dinner.

Fresh Mexican Salsa... Olé!

Makes about 2 cups

3 large or 4 medium Roma tomatoes, quartered
1/2 of a small onion, coarsely chopped
3 garlic cloves, crushed with the blade of knife
1 jalapeno, coarsely chopped and seeds removed (if you like spice leave some seeds but be careful!)
1/4 cup fresh cilantro, stems removed
1 teaspoon or more of salt
1/2 tsp pepper

Put all the ingredients into a food processor or blender and pulse until your desired consistency is achieved. Store in the refrigerator.

Serve with tortilla chips and Awesome Guacamole *(Hors d'Oeuvres)*, CauliWally Tacos, Veggie Fajitas or Jackfruit Tacos. *(Main Courses)*

Eat Your Vegetables, Bitches

Mango Salsa

Makes about 2 cups

1 ripe mango, peeled and finely diced
1 jalapeno pepper, finely diced, seeds removed
1/2 small red onion, finely diced
2 Roma tomatoes, finely diced
Juice of 1 lime

Combine all ingredients together, tossing gently. If you like a little spice, leave some of the seeds in the jalapeno, but be careful! A few seeds go a long way!

Spoon over grilled tofu or as a dip for tortilla chips!

Meatless Sauce with a Boost

Serves 6

Your children will never know that this "meat" sauce is loaded with super nutritious cauliflower!

---

1 TBLS olive oil
1 medium onion, chopped
1/4 to 1/3 head of cauliflower, finely chopped or 2 cups Cauliflower Rice
     (Costco sells frozen organic Cauliflower Rice)
1 package TJ's Beefless Ground Beef or your favorite beefless ground
2-3 TBLS of garlic, minced
1 TBLS dried oregano
1 TBLS dried basil
Or 2 TBLS dried Italian herbs
Salt and freshly ground pepper
A good splash of red wine
2-28 ounce cans of organic diced tomatoes, run some or all through the blender
1/2 - 1 cup vegetable broth
2 TBLS tomato paste

Put the cauliflower florets in a food processor with the shredding/grating attachment and process, the consistency of rice. Or, use a hand chopper. In a large sauté pan, heat 1 TBLS of olive oil over medium-high heat, then add the chopped onion and cook, stirring for 3 to 4 minutes, until just becoming translucent. Add the grated cauliflower and cook for about 3 minutes. Add the Beefless ground beef, breaking up as it cooks.

Over high heat, add the garlic, herbs, salt and pepper and the wine and cook for about 1 minute. Add the tomatoes, vegetable broth and tomato paste, stir. Reduce the heat to low and cover. Cook for about 30 minutes stirring a couple of times.

Serve over gluten free, whole wheat pasta or Zucchini Noodles.

*You can also make this Pomodoro with a Boost. Just use the Pomodoro Sauce *(Sauces and Such)* recipe and add the chopped cauliflower rice when you add in the garlic and herbs.

Finger Lickin' Peanut Sauce

Makes about 1 cup

This recipe is super easy and can be used for a dip or a dressing.
You may want to thin it a little with some rice vinegar if you use it for a salad dressing.

1/3 cup smooth peanut butter
2 TBLS liquid aminos or soy sauce
1 TBLS olive oil
1 TBLS sesame oil
1 tsp tamarind paste or concentrate
2 TBLS rice wine vinegar

3 TBLS lime juice
1/2 tsp Sriracha (more for spicy)
1 TBLS fresh ginger, peeled and chopped
3 cloves garlic, peeled and chopped
2 TBLS maple syrup or honey

Into the blender or food processor goes everything! Blend until everything is creamy and silky smooth.

Serve with Crispy Baked Tofu *(Hors d'Oeuvres)*, add to a stir-fry or as a dressing on your favorite salad greens.

Salads and Whatnot

Eat Your Vegetables, Bitches

Salads and Whatnot

A beautiful salad can go a long way to impress lunch or dinner guests. I have always gotten compliments on my salads and the reality is they are often just simple, but beautifully arranged. A word about the simplicity of salad: A weekly preparation of salad ingredients will make your Plant-Based life easier. Once a week dedicate a few of hours to planning, shopping and preparing food for the week. In the realm of salad, you can chop cucumbers, peppers, onions, beets, zucchini, fennel and put them in glass jars, roast chunks of sweet potato, make a big batch of Lemony Broccoli, roast vegetables of your choice, make quinoa, prepare your favorite tofu recipes. This way you will have salad ingredients for the week! Just add greens and your favorite dressing!

My Classic Dinner Salad

Serves 4

5 cups coarsely chopped romaine and red lettuce
1 cup cucumber, peeled with stripes and sliced
1/2 cup red onion, thinly sliced
1 cup cherry or grape tomatoes, halved

1/2 cup kalamata olives, halved
1/4 cup dried cranberries
Salt and pepper
1/3 cup vinaigrette of your choice

Wash, spin dry and coarsely chop the lettuce. Put the lettuce in a bowl with the cucumber, red onion and tomatoes and toss with the dressing. Don't drench the lettuce! Divide the salad onto 4 salad plates. Top with the olives and a sprinkle of dried cranberries, salt and pepper.

Italian Kale Salad

Makes 2 big or 4 small salads

I love kale! It is super nutritious and versatile. Salads, chips, soups and sautés…any way I can get kale, I will eat it! I like to chop the kale fairly small for this salad. And massage well!
Trust me, you're gonna love it!

6 cups of dinosaur kale, tightly packed, stems and ribs removed and finely chopped
Juice of 1 lemon
3 TBLS olive oil
2-3 garlic cloves, pressed
Salt and pepper, to taste
1/4 - 1 tsp crushed red pepper flakes, to taste (optional)
2/3 cup finely grated vegan parmesan or Pecorino Romano cheese OR a good sprinkle of Nutritional Yeast
2 cups freshly made Rootin' Tootin' Crootins *(Salads and Whatnot)*

Wash your hands. In a small bowl, whisk together the lemon juice, olive oil, garlic, salt, pepper and red pepper flakes. Pour over the kale in a large bowl and mix by hand, squeezing the kale a little to slightly bruise, this helps the dressing absorb the tough kale.

Add the nutritional yeast or vegan cheese and toss again. Allow to sit for 5 minutes for the flavors to exchange then toss with the croutons. Add a little extra pepper, if you are like me!
*Add chopped cabbage or dried cranberries for a little something extra!

Eat Your Vegetables, Bitches

Greek Salad in the Round

Serves 4

Presentation is everything! Well, it helps if things taste amazing, as well!
This is a beautifully delicious salad!

4 TBLS olive oil
4 TBLS fresh lemon juice
1 clove garlic, pressed
Salt and Freshly ground pepper
1 head romaine lettuce
4 Roma tomatoes, sliced
1 cucumber, sliced
1 small green pepper, cut in half, core and seeds removed, sliced into thin strips
1 small red pepper, cut in half, core and seeds removed, sliced into thin strips
1 small red onion, sliced
3/4 cup Kalamata olives
8 Pepperoncini

Combine the olive oil, lemon juice, garlic, salt and pepper in a small bowl.

Slice the romaine crosswise about a 1/2 inch thick, so it is shredded. Wash the romaine and spin dry or use a paper towel. In a large bowl place the shredded romaine and drizzle with 6 TBLS of the dressing. Toss well and put the salad greens on a round plate at least 12 inches in diameter, or in a large shallow bowl.

Slice the tomatoes 1/4 inch thick and place them on the lettuce towards the outside of the plate in a circle, overlapping about 1/3 of each tomato.

With a peeler, peel strips of skin off the cucumber, leaving 1/2 inch in between, so the cucumber has stripes! Slice the cucumber 1/4 inch thick and place slices in an overlapping circle inside the tomatoes.

Arrange the green and red peppers, red onion, kalamata olives and pepperoncini peppers in the middle. Drizzle with the remaining dressing and sprinkle with salt and pepper.

Serve with Dolmades, Spanakopita, *(Main Courses)* Baked Greek Veggies *(Green Things, Yellow Things...)* or just some good crusty bread!

Sesame Asian Cabbage Slaw

Serves 4

I believe cabbage is my favorite vegetable. You can go so many ways with cabbage.
And, in my mind the taste of sesame is Out of this World!
This salad is super fresh and tangy Yummers.

2 cups green cabbage, finely sliced
1 cup purple cabbage, finely sliced
1 cup carrots, shredded
1/2 red onion, thinly sliced

1 cup edamame
1/3 cup slivered almonds
1/3 cup Sesame Dressing *(Salad Dressings)*

Toss everything together and serve with your favorite Asian dishes, veggie burgers, or Carrot Dogs *(Main Courses)*.

Arugula, Spinach, Fennel & Strawberry Salad

4 small or 2 large salads

We had a version of this in Maui, and I vowed to recreate.

2 cups tightly packed arugula
2 cups tightly packed spinach
1/2 cup thinly sliced fennel
1 cup strawberries, sliced
1/3 cup of Balsamic & Lemon Vinaigrette or
    Sweet Balsamic Vinaigrette *(Salad Dressings)*

1/4 cup toasted pine nuts
Vegan goat cheese, optional *(Hors d'Oeuvres)*
Freshly ground pepper

Put the arugula, spinach and fennel in a large salad bowl. Drizzle the Balsamic & Lemon Vinaigrette over the greens and gently toss to combine. Divide the salad onto two or four plates. Scatter the strawberries and pine nuts on top and finish with freshly ground pepper and a dollop of vegan goat cheese.

A Wedge of Greece

Serves 4

People will be Wowed with this one!

For the salad:
2 heads of romaine lettuce
1 1/2 cups cherry tomatoes, halved
1 cup cucumber, cut in half, seeded and diced in 1/2 inch chunks
1/2 cup celery, diced in 1/2 inch chunks
1/2 cup Kalamata olives, halved
1/2 medium red onion, thinly sliced
1 TBLS fresh lemon juice

For the dressing:
1/4 cup extra virgin olive oil
4 TBLS fresh lemon juice
2 rounded TBLS of tahini
3 cloves garlic, pressed
1/4 tsp salt
2 TBLS fresh mint, chopped
Freshly ground pepper
A scatter of finely chopped mint

Wash and cut the heads of romaine in half lengthwise, all the way down through the end, leaving the bottom so they make an intact wedge.

In a mixing bowl add the cherry tomatoes, cucumber, celery, olives, red onion, lemon juice and a dash of salt and pepper. Toss well.

For the dressing, add all the ingredients into a small bowl and whisk to combine. Adjust the salt, lemon and garlic for your taste. Set aside.

Place one romaine half on each plate, cut side up. Divide the tomato salad evenly over each wedge.

Spoon drizzle the dressing lightly over each salad. Top with freshly chopped mint and pepper.

Un-Traditional Caesar Salad

Serves 4

What can I say…Caesar Salad, Baby!
A word about Worcestershire Sauce: Typically it contains anchovies or fish sauce,
so it does not fall in the category of vegan.
However, you can find vegan Worcestershire made by Annie's or The Wizard's.

1 large head fresh, crisp romaine lettuce
1 packed cup kale, stems removed and finely chopped
1/4 cup vegan mayo
2 large cloves garlic, pressed
Juice of 1 small lemon
Salt and pepper
1 TBLS vegan Worcestershire sauce

Several dashes Tabasco sauce
1/2 cup fresh grated vegan Parmesan cheese or
2 TBLS nutritional yeast
1/4 cup extra virgin olive oil

1 recipe Rootin' Tootin' Crootins
(Salads and Whatnot)

Holding the head of lettuce together, cut off the end and cut the romaine into 1 inch slices. Wash and spin dry. Put the romaine into a large salad bowl. Remove the stems from the kale and finely chop. Toss the kale in with the romaine, cover with a tea towel and keep cool in the refrigerator.

In a blender add vegan mayo, garlic, juice of one lemon, salt, pepper, Worcestershire, Tabasco and half of the vegan Parmesan or nutritional yeast. Blend on low as you slowly add the olive oil. Taste and add more olive oil or lemon juice, salt or pepper…whatever it needs.

Drizzle half of the Caesar dressing over the romaine and toss. Add more dressing, as you need. Sprinkle with freshly ground pepper and vegan Parmesan cheese. Top with Rootin' Tootin' Crootins.

AKA: Croutons
Makes 2 cups

This recipe was named by my good friend Michael Simmons and my other good friend and
former band mate, Nathan December. They don't know this, and probably
don't remember the story from whence the name came.
(Don't you just love other people's inside jokes?
Right up there with listening to somebody tell you what they dreamt.)
Here goes: Our beloved friend Julie Lindon Perkins, may she rest in peace, was a great chef!
One night Julie was making croutons and when Nathan saw them he exclaimed, "Crootins!"
Enter Michael with the best response ever…"Rootin' Tootin' Crootins!"
And so they have been dubbed! This is my version of Julie's croutons.
I like to make a tidy sum of these because they are so delicious!
But, make them in batches of two cups each otherwise they will not get coated well
with the olive oil and Earth Balance mixture.

---

2 cups of crusty Italian or French bread, cut into 1 inch cubes
1+TBLS olive oil
1+ TBSP Earth Balance
Granulated Garlic

Cut the bread into 1inch cubes. First, spray a large sauté pan or skillet with olive oil or canola spray,
then melt the Earth Balance with the olive oil over medium-high heat. Swirl the oil mixture to cover the entire pan. Add the bread cubes and toss with two spoons to completely coat. Give a good
sprinkle of granulated garlic to cover cubes, toss again and give another sprinkle. Add more olive oil
and Earth Balance, if necessary, to coat. Reduce heat to medium and allow to them cook untouched
for two minutes. Begin turning each crouton over to lightly brown on another side. Allow them to
cook for two more minutes. Toss with the spoons and cook for a couple more minutes, or until nice
and lightly brown.

Serve with salads, soups, pasta or just eat them!

Mediterranean Quinoa Salad

Serves 4

Quinoa is such a cool grain! Actually, it is a grain grown for its seeds.
It is a plant food high in protein, rich in vitamins and minerals, gluten free, a great source
of fiber and contains all nine amino acids. Wow! What does that mean to you?
Protein is made up of amino acids, nine of them are called essential because our
body cannot produce them, so we need to get them from foods. A food that contains
all nine amino acids is known as a complete protein.
In other words quinoa is an Awesome protein!
And so versatile and delicious!

1 cup quinoa, uncooked
1/2 tsp salt
1 cup cucumber, seeded, diced and unpeeled
1 cup green pepper, diced
2 cups diced tomatoes, without juice
1 cup Kalamata olives, halved
1/2 cup chopped red onion
Juice of 1 lemon
2 TBLS olive oil
1 clove garlic, pressed
2 tsp each granulated garlic, dried oregano, dried basil
1/4 tsp salt
Pepper to taste

Rinse and cook quinoa according to package directions, adding the 1/2 tsp salt.

Meanwhile, combine cucumber, green pepper, tomatoes, olives, onion, lemon juice, olive oil, garlic
and the herbs in large bowl, toss and set aside.

Allow the quinoa to cool completely. Add quinoa to vegetable mixture; toss gently to combine. Taste
and adjust the seasonings.

Serve immediately or refrigerate until cold.

*Quinoa typically is found in the rice and pasta section of supermarkets. Rinse well before cooking
to remove the natural bitter coating.

*Quinoa can be cooked the day before and stored in a sealed container in the refrigerator, if desired.

Eat Your Vegetables, Bitches

Antipasto Salad

Serves 4 - 6

Oh Lord! There is something so special about Antipasto! Antipasto is a traditional first course in an Italian meal. Ever diverse, and depending on the region, Antipasto can be anything from cured meats, cheeses, hard or soft, marinated veggies, salted fish, olives and peppers.

When I was in my early 20's I worked at an Italian restaurant in Studio City, California called Georgio's. Coming from Texas I had NO idea what Antipasto was.
At Georgio's they served Antipasto as a salad, and it was delicious.
This is my veganized version of the Antipasto Salad at Georgio's.

Note: Most grocery stores have an Olive Bar where you can buy olives, marinated peppers, artichoke hearts and mushrooms. Personally, I like to make my own marinated mushrooms, but you can simplify your life at the Olive Bar!

1/3 cup Olive Oil + 1 TBLS
1/3 cup Red Wine Vinegar
3 cloves garlic, pressed
1 TBLS lemon juice
Salt and pepper to taste
1 cup marinated mushrooms
      (1 1/2 cups raw mushrooms,
      if you are making your own)
1 cup grilled zucchini

1 large head romaine lettuce, chopped
1 cup grape tomatoes, halved
1 cup cucumber, peeled leaving stripes,
      cut in quarters lengthwise and
      cut into chunks
1 cup mixed olives
1 cup marinated peppers
1 cup marinated artichoke hearts
1/2 cup red onion, thinly sliced

Combine the olive oil, red wine vinegar, 2 cloves of pressed garlic, lemon juice, salt and pepper in a jar with a lid. Shake well and set aside.

Slice the mushrooms. Heat a skillet with 1 TBLS olive oil then add the mushrooms. Sauté for about 2-3 minutes, just until beginning to get soft. Remove from the pan into a small bowl. Over the mushrooms, press 1 clove of garlic, add 1 tsp olive oil, 1 TBLS red wine vinegar, 1/4 tsp crushed red pepper, a dash of Italian herbs, salt and pepper. Mix well and refrigerate.

Cut the ends off of a large zucchini, cut into 1/4 inch rounds, brush with olive oil, sprinkle with pepper and a little salt and grill over medium high heat until you have grill marks on both sides, or in a cast iron skillet until becoming a bit charred. Set aside to cool.

Arrange the chopped romaine lettuce on a large flat plate or a big shallow salad bowl. Arrange "piles" of tomatoes, cucumber, olives, mushrooms, peppers, zucchini, artichoke hearts and red onion on top of the lettuce. Sprinkle with pepper. Just before serving shake the red wine vinegar dressing well and drizzle all over the salad.

Serve with crusty Italian bread!

Panzanella a la Rootin' Tootin' Crootins!

Serves 4-6

I know, it sounds kind of Redneck, but hey, I grew up in Texas, so I'm allowed! These croutons are so amazingly scrumptious, why not add them to a delicious Greek salad and call it Panzanella!

1 recipe of Rootin' Tootin' Crootins *(Salads and Whatnot)*
1/2 - 3/4 cup of Greek Vinaigrette *(Salad Dressings)*
1 cucumber, 4 strips peeled to leave stripes,
      cut in quarters lengthwise and cut into chunks
2 cups grape or cherry tomatoes, halved
1 red bell pepper, diced large

1 green bell pepper, diced large
1/2 red onion, sliced in thin half rounds
1 cup pitted Kalamata olives, halved
Fresh chopped basil
Pepper and salt

Put the cucumbers, tomatoes, red peppers, green peppers and onion in a large bowl. Pour the vinaigrette over the veggies and mix well.

Add in the Kalamata olives and croutons. Mix well. Sprinkle with fresh basil, pepper and taste before adding salt.

Asian Tofu Bowl

Serves 4

Bowls are a fantastic way to have a healthy lunch or dinner on the go. I have given you two "Bowl" recipes, in two different serving sizes, and just like Smoothies you can mix and match and be uber creative in the Realm of Bowls!

---

1 recipe Asian Tofu *(Main Courses)*
2 cups Lemony Broccoli
    (Green Things, Yellow Things…)
2 cups cucumber, seeded and diced
2 cups spinach sautéed with garlic…
    …it takes about 2 pounds of fresh spinach to cook
    down to 2 cups or use 1-10 ounce package frozen
    spinach sautéed with garlic.

2 cups diced red pepper
    (Really, any veggies,
    cooked or raw that you like)
1 cup quinoa, uncooked
4 TBLS Fresh basil, chopped
Garlic Dijon Dressing
    (Salad Dressings)

Rinse and cook the quinoa to the package directions. Allow to cool.

Sauté the spinach: Add 2 TBLS water or 1 TBLS olive oil to a large sauté pan and heat over medium high. Toss in the spinach and cook until beginning to wilt, then add the garlic and cook stirring for about 1 more minute. Bring the heat up to high for a minute to evaporate excess liquid. Season with pepper and a little salt.

Divide the cooled quinoa into the bottom of 4 individual bowls. In sections, put 1/2 cup of each: tofu, broccoli, spinach, red pepper and cucumber. Drizzle with Garlic Dijon Dressing and sprinkle each bowl with 1 TBLS chopped basil.

Vegan Power Bowl

Serves 2

Another delicious combination! This is a Power Bowl because it is full of health promoting, power foods! Avocado is a wonderful source of plant-based fats and nutrients, sweet potato is loaded with anti-oxidants, vitamins and minerals, Spring Greens…well, Green Food!
Pumpkin seeds are a great source of protein, omega 3 fatty acids vitamins and minerals and blueberries are one of the most nutrient dense foods on the planet!
Powerful!

1 avocado	2 TBLS raw pumpkin seeds
1 sweet potato	1 cup fresh blueberries
1/2 cup red onion, thinly sliced	Salt & pepper
4 handfuls of Spring Greens	1/4 – 1/3 cup Lemon Tahini Dressing *(Salad Dressings)*
1 cup cooked quinoa	

Rinse and cook the quinoa to the package directions. Allow to cool.

Peel and cube the sweet potato, Toss with 1/2 TBLS olive oil and roast at 375 degrees for about 20-25 minutes. Allow to cool.

Toss the spring greens with the Lemon Tahini Dressing. In two bowls, divide the spring greens. In quadrants put 1/2 cup quinoa, 1/2 cup fresh blueberries, cubed sweet potatoes, and 1/2 an avocado scooped out, sliced and "fanned" out! Sprinkle with sliced red onion, raw pumpkin seeds, pepper and salt.

Eat Your Vegetables, Bitches

Quinoa Tabbouleh ~ Gluten Free

Serves 4 - 6

The salad version!

---

1 bunch curly parsley	1-2 cups diced fresh tomatoes, juice strained
1 cup uncooked quinoa	1 lemon, juiced
4 green onions, diced	1/4 cup extra virgin olive oil
2-4 TBLS chopped fresh mint	Salt and freshly ground pepper

To cook the quinoa: Add 1 cup of rinsed quinoa to 2 cups of boiling water. Stir, turn heat down to low and cover. Check after 10 minutes. Cook until the water is absorbed. Fluff with a fork and cool.

Pick parsley leaves off and wash thoroughly ~ No Stems. Dry the parsley well. Chop the parsley very fine and put into a big bowl. Add one cup of completely cooled quinoa and mix gently. Add more quinoa to your liking. Find the parsley/quinoa combination that suits you!

Add green onions, mint and tomatoes. Add as much or as little of the tomatoes as your taste dictates. I like LOTS of tomatoes!

Juice the lemon and combine with the olive oil. Pour over the parsley mixture a little at a time, mixing to a consistency that is not too wet. You may not use it all. Add salt and pepper to taste.

You can play with this recipe adding more or less of any of the ingredients. Have fun with it!

Serve on a bed of lettuce dressed with a simple oil and vinegar and pita or with gluten free crackers, olives and hummus.

Eat Your Vegetables, Bitches

Fruit Salad with Fresh Herbs

Serves 4

It wouldn't be summer without fresh fruit. The fresh herbs and lime give this salad a little something extra! The great thing about making fruit salad is you can use whatever fruits you have on hand. I have made some suggestions, but feel free to mix and match with what you have in your kitchen. Serve this as a starter for Brunch, or as an afternoon treat on a hot day.

2 cups strawberries, sliced	1 TBLS fresh mint, finely chopped
2 cups watermelon, 1inch chunks	1 TBLS fresh basil, finely chopped
1 cup fresh blueberries	1 lime
1 cup grapes, red, green or mixed, cut in half	Mint leaves for garnish
2 cups peach or nectarine, chunks	

Wash and cut up all the fruit and toss gently to mix. Sprinkle on the mint and basil, squeeze half of the lime and toss gently. Taste and add more herbs and or lime juice, if you desire.

Serve this salad with Brunch, topped with some of my Gluten Free Granola *(Breakfast of Champions)* and garnish with fresh mint.

Spicy Cabbage Slaw

Serves 4

The crunch of cabbage, the tang of lime and the spice of Sriracha will send your taste buds to the moon! Adjust the amounts of mayo, Sriracha and lime depending on how creamy, spicy and tangy you like your Slaw!

1/2 small head green cabbage, thinly sliced	1-2 TBLS Sriracha
1/4 small head purple cabbage, thinly sliced	1 lime, juiced
1/2 cup red onion, finely diced	1/2 tsp pepper
3/4 cup vegan mayo	Salt to taste

In a small bowl, combine the vegan mayo, Sriracha and lime juice. Stir well. In a big bowl, combine the two cabbages and red onion. Pour the dressing over and mix well. Add pepper and stir lightly. Taste and adjust flavors.

Serve with CauliWally Tacos, JackFruit Tacos, Carrot Dogs *(Main Courses)* or as a side to any Curry dish.

Salad Dressings

Eat Your Vegetables, Bitches

Salads Dressings

Greek Vinaigrette

Makes about 1 cup

1/4 cup red wine vinegar
1/4 cup lemon juice
2 garlic cloves, pressed
1 teaspoon dried oregano
1 heaping teaspoon Dijon mustard
1/2 teaspoon salt
Freshly ground pepper
1/2 cup of olive oil

In a small bowl, whisk together the vinegar, lemon, garlic, oregano, mustard, salt and pepper. Continue whisking while you slowly pour in the olive oil.

Store in the refrigerator.

Poppyseed Vinaigrette

Makes about 1 cup

My friend Mary Miranda gave me this recipe years ago.
I am not sure if it is still intact, but it is close! Thanks Mary!

---

1 TBLS finely grated onion and juice
1 TBLS honey
1 tsp dry mustard
1 tsp salt
3/4 cup canola oil
1/3 cup apple cider vinegar
1 1/2 tablespoons Poppy Seeds

Mix all ingredients except oil and Poppy Seeds in a blender. Slowly add the oil while the blender is running. Pour into a glass jar. Gently stir in the Poppy Seeds and refrigerate.

This dressing is wonderful on a simple salad made of Romaine lettuce topped with sliced grapefruit, sliced avocado and toasted slivered almonds.

Eat Your Vegetables, Bitches

Balsamic & Lemon Vinaigrette

Makes about 1 1/4 cup

1/2 cup balsamic vinegar
1/4 cup freshly squeezed lemon juice
1 tsp finely grated lemon zest
1/2 tsp salt
Freshly ground pepper
1/2 cup extra virgin olive oil

In a bowl, combine the balsamic, lemon juice, lemon zest, salt and pepper.

While whisking, slowly pour the olive oil in and continue whisking until smooth.

Pour the vinaigrette in a jar with a lid. Shake well before using.

Store in the refrigerator.

Sweet Balsamic Dressing

Makes about 1 1/4 cup

1/2 cup olive oil
1/2 cup Balsamic Vinegar
1/4 cup real maple syrup

Mix well. Store in a glass jar in the refrigerator. That's it! Simple and so delicious!

Lemon Tahini Dressing

Makes about 1 cup

1/3 cup lemon juice
1/3 cup olive oil
1/3 cup tahini
1 TBLS honey
2 cloves garlic, pressed
1 tsp sea salt
1 tsp black pepper

Combine all the ingredients in the blender and mix well until nice and creamy.

Store in the refrigerator.

Garlic Dijon Dressing

Makes about 1 cup

"Look Ma, No Oil!"

1/2 cup of raw cashews, soaked
1 TBLS Dijon mustard
3 cloves garlic, chopped
Juice of 1 lemon
Soaking water
Salt and pepper

Boil 1 cup of water. Turn off the heat and add the cashews. Soak for 30 minutes. Drain, but save the soaking water. Put cashews, Dijon, garlic, lemon juice and 1/4 cup of the soaking water into a blender. Pulse until smooth, adding more water as needed. Season with pepper and more lemon, add salt if needed.

Sesame Dressing

Makes about 1 cup

1/2 cup Balsamic Vinegar
2 TBLS Maple Syrup
3 TBLS Sesame Oil
1 tsp Granulated Garlic
1/2 cup olive oil

Combine all the ingredients in a bottle or jar with a good lid and shake well before pouring.

Classic French Vinaigrette

You can double or triple this recipe and store in the refrigerator.

4 TBLS lemon juice
4 TBLS red wine vinegar
1/2 a shallot, finely diced
2 tsp Dijon mustard
1/3 cup olive oil
Salt and pepper

In a bowl, add the lemon juice, vinegar, shallot and mustard. Whisk well to combine. Slowly add the olive oil whisking quickly until it has thickened. Season with salt and pepper.

Taste and adjust.

Soups and Stews

Eat Your Vegetables, Bitches

Soups and Stews

Curry Cauliflower Soup

Serves 4 - 6

This is an unassuming soup! Be prepared to say, "Yum!"

---

1 TBLS olive oil
1 onion, chopped
2-3 cloves garlic, pressed
1 heaping tsp turmeric
2 heaping tsp garam masala
1 tsp cumin
1/8 or more tsp cayenne pepper
1/2 tsp salt and 1/2 tsp pepper

1 big carrot, peeled and sliced
4 cups cauliflower, cut into small florets
1/2 cup diced bell pepper, red or green
1 cup celery, chopped
4 cups vegetable broth
1 14 ounce can diced tomatoes
1 14 ounce can coconut milk
2-3 TBLS fresh cilantro, chopped

In a big pot, sauté the onions in the olive oil over medium heat for 5 minutes. Add the garlic, spices, salt and pepper and cook for 1 minute, stirring. Add the carrots, cauliflower, peppers and celery and cook for 3-5 minutes on medium. Add the vegetable broth and tomatoes, reduce heat to medium low, cover and simmer for about 30 minutes, stirring a couple of times. Add the coconut milk, heat through and serve with chopped cilantro.

Eat Your Vegetables, Bitches

Lisa's Delicious Vegetable Soup!

Serves 4

The wonderful thing about vegetable soup is you can add whatever veggies you have on hand.
Follow this recipe as it is or mix and match veggies!

Olive Oil or Canola Oil Spray
1 medium onion, diced
2 cloves garlic, pressed
1 large zucchini, diced
2 celery stalks, diced
2 carrots, peeled and diced
2 cups broccoli florets
Lots of mushrooms! sliced (if you like them)
        So many health benefits!

1 red or green pepper, diced
1/4 of a head of cabbage, sliced
2-3 handfuls of chopped kale, ribs removed
1- 14oz can diced tomatoes
4-5 cups of vegetable broth
1 TBLS Italian herbs
Salt and pepper to taste

Spray a large pot and heat over medium high heat. Add the onions and sauté for a few minutes until becoming translucent. Toss in all the veggies and garlic, stirring for two minutes then add the broth, canned tomatoes and Italian herbs. Bring to a boil over high heat, reduce to low and simmer covered for about 30-40 minutes.

Feel free to add a can of kidney beans and 1/2 cup of small, uncooked pasta to transform your soup into Minestrone!

Sprinkle your bowl of soup with Gomasio!

"Cream" of Zucchini Soup

Serves 4

At the height of summer, when everyone is begging you to please take some zucchini from their garden…Take it! And make this amazingly simple soup.

---

4 large zucchinis, cut into 1 inch cubes
1 medium onion, coarsely chopped
3-4 cloves of garlic, coarsely chopped

2 cups vegetable broth, for steaming and thinning
1/2 cup coconut milk
Salt and pepper

Pour the 2 cups of vegetable broth in a big pot with a steamer basket. Place the cut zucchini, onion and garlic in the basket, turn the heat on high, cover and steam for about 12 minutes. The zucchini should be very soft.

Allow the zucchini and onion to cool for 10-15 minutes. Put the zucchini, onions, garlic and 1/2 cup of the broth into the blender or food processor and process until smooth. Add more vegetable broth, if necessary, to thin. Transfer to a pot, add the coconut milk and heat through.

*Bonus- Use this yummy recipe to make "Cream" of Broccoli, "Cream" of Cauliflower or "Cream" of Asparagus by substituting a big head of broccoli, a medium head of cauliflower or a large bunch of trimmed asparagus!

Tomato Basil Soup

Serves 4

Another summertime favorite! There is nothing more delicious than tomato soup made with perfectly ripe tomatoes in the summer. Except for perhaps when you pull some fresh tomato soup out of the freezer in November or December! Double or triple this recipe and freeze!

1 TBLS olive oil
3 pounds ripe tomatoes, cut in big chunks
    OR 3-14.5 ounce cans of diced tomatoes
1 medium onion, chopped
5 cloves of garlic, chopped

1/3 cup fresh basil packed and chopped
1 can full fat Coconut Milk - 13.5 ounces
Salt and pepper
2 TBLS fresh basil, cut in ribbons

Heat the olive oil in a big pot over medium high heat. Put the tomatoes, onions and garlic into the pot and stir well. Reduce heat to medium and cook down until the tomatoes begin to disintegrate, stirring occasionally, about 20 minutes. Add salt and pepper. Remove from heat and allow to cool for about 30 minutes. Add the coconut milk and basil and put into the blender or food processor. Blend until smooth. Adjust the seasoning.

Stack 5 basil leaves, roll up from stem to tip and cut into ribbons.

Top each bowl with a sprinkle of chopped fresh basil. Enjoy!

Eat Your Vegetables, Bitches

The BEST Butternut Squash Soup!

Serves 4 - 6

I love this recipe! My friend, Joe Illig makes this soup and the first time I tasted it I was in Autumn Heaven! I don't know where Joe got the recipe, but I have altered it a bit and made it vegan! It is so fun to make, too! It's like a science project...but not too time intensive!
I know you will enjoy!

---

2 TBLS Earth Balance
2 medium shallots, finely chopped (about 4 TBLS)
1 large Butternut Squash, washed, unpeeled,
     cut in half lengthwise, seeds and stringy fibers scraped
     out and reserved, then cut each half into quarters
6 cups vegetable broth
1/2 tsp salt
1 – 14 oz can full fat coconut milk
Fresh chives, chopped

In a large Dutch oven or large stock pot, heat the Earth Balance over medium heat until beginning to foam. Add the shallots and cook, stirring until softened, about 3 minutes. Add the seeds and scrapings from the squash and cook stirring occasionally until it turns a nice saffron color, about 4 minutes.

Add 1/2 tsp salt, the 6 cups of vegetable broth and stir. Bring to a boil over high heat, then reduce heat to medium-low. Place a steamer basket in the Dutch oven and arrange the squash cut-side down in the steamer basket. Cover and steam until the squash is very tender, about 35-40 minutes. Puncture the squash with a knife to make sure it is tender.

Remove from heat and transfer the squash to a rimmed baking sheet and allow to cool, reserving the steaming liquid. When cool enough to handle, use a large spoon to scrape all the flesh out of the skin (that sounds morbid!) and into a medium bowl. Compost the skin.

Pour the reserved steaming liquid through a mesh strainer into a second bowl; compost the solids. Wipe out any bits from the Dutch oven with a paper towel.

Purée the squash and reserved liquid in a blender or food processor in several batches. You may not need all the liquid. You want the soup to be thickish. Transfer the puréed soup back to the Dutch oven. Stir in the coconut milk and heat over medium-low until hot.

Garnish with fresh chopped chives and/or Rootin' Tootin' Crootins' *(Salads and Whatnot)*!

Crockpot Vegetable Lentil Soup

Serves 6

1 - 16 oz bag brown lentils
8 cups vegetable broth
1 - 15 oz can Fire Roasted tomatoes
2 medium potatoes, diced
1 large carrot, sliced
2 stalks celery, sliced
1 zucchini, diced

1/4 head of cabbage, sliced
1 large onion, diced
2 cloves garlic, chopped
1/2 TBLS Italian Herbs
1 tsp salt
1 tsp pepper
2 cups fresh kale, stems removed and chopped

Add all the ingredients to the crockpot, except the kale. Cook on Low for 8 hours.

Add the kale and cook for 15 minutes or until your desired tenderness.

Enjoy!

Split Pea Soup

Makes a big pot and serves about 6

Chrissie loves Pea Soup! This one is for you, Miss Kylo Girl!

1 - 1 lb. bag green or yellow split peas, rinsed
Olive oil or canola spray
1 large yellow onion, diced
3 garlic cloves, minced
2 medium carrots, peeled and sliced
2 stalks celery, cut in half lengthwise and diced

6-8 cups vegetable broth
2 tsp dried thyme
1 tsp smoked paprika
2 bay leaves
Salt and pepper

Sort and rinse the split peas. Spray a large pot and heat over medium high. Add the diced onions and cook stirring for about 4-5 minutes, until golden. Add the carrots and celery and cook for 2-3 minutes. Add the garlic and stir for 1 minute. Add the split peas, 6 cups of vegetable broth, dried thyme, smoked paprika, bay leaves and pepper. Bring to a boil. Reduce heat to medium low, stir, cover and simmer for 45 minutes to 1 hour, until the peas are soft. Stir occasionally, adding more broth if the soup gets too thick. Taste and add salt and more pepper, if necessary.

Garnish with chopped fresh thyme.

Easy Black Bean Soup

Serves 4 - 6

Emphasis on the Easy!

Olive oil or canola spray
1 medium onion, finely diced
3 cloves garlic, pressed
3 cans of black beans, drained
5 cups vegetable broth
1 – 14.5 ounce can diced tomatoes
1 – 4 ounce can green chilies
1 TBLS dried oregano
2 tsp cumin
2 tsp chili powder
1/4 – 1 tsp crushed red pepper
Salt and pepper to taste
Vegan sour cream or Plain vegan yogurt and chopped chives for garnish

---

Spray a big pot and heat over medium high. Add the onions and cook stirring until becoming translucent. Add the garlic and cook stirring for one minute. Add the black beans, vegetable broth, tomatoes, green chilis, oregano, cumin, chili powder and red pepper. Bring to a boil, reduce heat to medium low, cover and simmer for 20 minutes. Taste and add salt and pepper, if necessary.

Ladle into bowls and top with a dollop of vegan plain yogurt or sour cream and a sprinkle of chopped chives.

As always, the soup will be most excellent the next day, so make ahead, if possible!

Quick Killer Chili

Serves 6

I made this up on a whim one afternoon when we suddenly had a few people coming over to watch the Seahawks game. It was gone before the game ended!
Mic Drop.

---

1 TBLS olive oil
1 medium yellow onion, chopped
1/2 - 1 tsp crushed red pepper or more if you like it spicy!
4 cloves garlic, chopped
1 medium green pepper, big dice
1 medium red pepper, big dice
1 package Trader Joe's Beefless Ground Beef
2 –14.5 ounce cans diced tomatoes
2 cups vegetable broth
1 -15 ounce can pinto beans, drained
1 -15 ounce can kidney beans, drained
1 -15 ounce can corn, drained
3 TBLS chili powder
1 Heaping TBLS cumin
1 TBLS Italian herbs
Salt and pepper

In a big pot heat the olive oil over high heat. Add the onions and reduce heat to medium high, stirring until the onions are translucent, about 5 minutes. Add the red and green peppers and cook for about 4 minutes. Add the garlic and stir for 1 minute. Add the Beefless Ground Beef breaking it up as you stir. Add the remaining ingredients, stir well and simmer for 20 minutes. Taste and adjust seasonings.

Serve with corn bread or tortilla chips, chopped onions and sliced avocado on top!

Mushroom Stew

Serves 4

I used to be a meat eater. I was born and raised in Texas and I grew up eating meat.
Roast beef, fried chicken, Mexican food, fried fish and whatever my brothers brought home from
hunting at the ranch. And, then there was Beef Stew. What a wonderful invention, Stew!
Fast forward to the present and swap out the beef for nutrient dense mushrooms and the rest is
history! Mushrooms are a great substitute for meat. If you brown them up and allow the flavors to
mingle you will have a delicious pot of comfort food on a cold night!

---

1 TBLS olive oil
6 cups mushrooms, cut in big chunks
1 large onion, diced
5 garlic cloves, minced
1/2 cup dry red wine
3 medium potatoes, peeled and cut in chunks
2 carrots, peeled and cut in chunks
3 celery stalks, cut in chunks
1 – 14 oz can diced tomatoes, with juice
4 cups vegetable broth
1 bay leaf
1 TBLS dried Italian herbs
1 tsp thyme
1/2 tsp salt
1/2 tsp pepper

Heat the olive oil in a deep pot over medium high heat. Add the mushrooms and onions stirring often, until nicely browned, about 10 minutes. Add in the garlic and stir constantly for about one minute. Turn the heat up to high and add in the red wine, cooking for 1 minute and scraping up the bits on the bottom of the pot. Add in the potatoes, carrots, celery, tomatoes, broth, bay leaf, herbs, salt and pepper. Bring to a boil then reduce heat to low, cover and simmer for about 20-25 minutes. Check to see if potatoes and carrots are soft but firm. Taste and adjust seasonings.

Serve in a bowl on its own, over Mashed Cauliflower or eggless noodles with a green salad on the side and a hunk of warm crusty Italian bread. Perfection!

Hungarian Mushroom Soup

Serves 4

I first had this type of soup in 2006 at PCC, our local co-op. Then my friend Heather Mitchell gave me a similar recipe, as we bonded over us both being foodies!
I have altered that recipe a bit, and of course Veganized it!
It's Delicious! You can serve this on its own, with a hunk of crusty bread,
over eggless noodles or with a scoop of quinoa!

Olive oil or canola spray
1 large yellow onion, chopped
12 ounces fresh mushrooms, sliced
1 heaping tsp dried dill
2 cups vegetable broth, divided
1 TBLS Bragg's Liquid Aminos, Tamari or soy sauce
1 TBLS paprika
2 TBLS Earth Balance
3 TBLS flour or corn starch
1 - 14 ounce can coconut milk
1/2 a lemon, juiced
Salt and pepper
Fresh dill, chopped
1/2 cup vegan plain yogurt or vegan sour cream

Spray a large pot and heat over medium high. Add the onions and cook stirring for about 4 minutes, until they are becoming translucent. Add the sliced mushrooms, dill, 1/2 cup of vegetable broth, Bragg's or Tamari, and paprika. Stir well, cover and simmer for 15 minutes on medium low.

Meanwhile…

In a separate pot melt the Earth Balance over medium high heat. Whisk in the flour or corn starch and cook, whisking for 1 minute. Add the coconut milk and the remaining 1 1/2 cups vegetable broth and whisk well over medium low heat for about 10 minutes.

Pour the milk mixture into the mushrooms and bring the heat up to boil. Reduce heat to low, cover and simmer for 10 minutes.

Remove from heat and add the lemon juice, pepper and a little salt. Taste and adjust seasonings. You may want more dill or lemon or pepper.

Serve with a dollop of vegan plain yogurt or vegan sour cream and a sprinkle of fresh dill!

Magical Mulligatawny

Serves 6

This soup is Magical!
I called my friend Karen Arnold one day, not knowing she had to have an emergency
appendectomy four days before. She answered the phone and it was immediately
apparent that she was not feeling well at all! She told me to talk to her, because she felt like crap
and didn't have the energy to talk. Well, about fifteen minutes into the conversation I noticed she
was talking to me and becoming more and more animated and energetic. I pointed this out to her,
and she said that while I had been talking, she had been eating a bowl of Mulligatawny Soup!
I had no idea what it was, but when she described the spices, I knew I had to have the recipe.
Mulligatawny Soup originates from South India, and there are many recipes and variations.
Here is my Veganized Instant Pot version! If you don't have an Instant Pot…Get One!
Or just follow the recipe and cook according to the directions below the Instant Pot directions.
P.S. I use heaping spoonsful of the spices! Do so, as well if you feel so inclined.

Olive oil or canola spray	1/2 tsp Nutmeg
2 TBLS Earth Balance	1/2 tsp Cinnamon
1 medium onion, diced	1/2 tsp dried thyme
3 stalks celery, diced	1/2 tsp salt
1 green pepper, seeded and diced	1/2 tsp pepper
2 carrots, peeled and sliced	6 cups vegetable broth
2 small zucchinis, cut in half and sliced in 1/2 inch chunks,	2 cans garbanzo beans, drained
2 cups broccoli florets	1 – 14.5 ounce can diced tomatoes
4 cloves garlic, finely chopped	1/2 cup basmati or jasmine rice
2 tsp fresh ginger, minced or 1/2 tsp ginger powder	1 apple, peeled and diced
2 TBLS yellow curry	3 whole cloves or 1/2 tsp ground cloves
2 tsp Garam Masala	1 can full fat coconut milk

Mise en place is a French expression meaning "everything in its place". So, when a chef says "mise en place", it means get everything prepared up front. With that in mind….

Cut up all the vegetables, measure out the spices and put them into one container, prepare the vegetable broth, open the tomatoes, rinse the garbanzo beans, measure out the rice…Mise en place!

Turn on the Instant Pot to Sauté mode, spray the bottom of the pot and add the Earth Balance. Add the onions, celery, green pepper, carrots, zucchini and broccoli. Cook stirring for 2 minutes. Stir in the garlic and ginger and cook for one minute.

Sprinkle on the spice mixture and stir well.

Add the vegetable broth and stir. Add the garbanzo beans, tomatoes, rice, apple and cloves, stir well. Put the lid on the Instant Pot and lock into place. Set the steam release valve to 'Sealing'.

Cancel the Sauté mode and press Manual (or pressure cook) button and the + to select 7 minutes.

When the cycle ends, allow to sit and naturally release pressure for about 20 minutes. Then turn the steam valve to 'Venting' to release the rest of the pressure.

When the pin on the lid drops, open the pot and stir.

Turn on the sauté mode and add the coconut milk. When it begins to bubble turn it off and stir.

Enjoy!

OR, If you do not have an Instant Pot:

Spray the bottom of a big stock pot, add the Earth Balance and heat over medium high. Add the veggies and cook stirring for about 5 minutes. Add the garlic and ginger, stir for 1 minute. Sprinkle on the spice mixture, stir. Add the vegetable broth, garbanzo beans, tomatoes, rice, apple and cloves. Stir and bring to a boil. Reduce heat to low and simmer covered for 30 minutes.

Add the coconut milk and simmer 5 minutes. Taste and adjust seasonings.

Green Immunity Soup

Makes about 4 quarts

If you were brought up on Chicken Soup for whatever ails you, you must try my Green Immunity Soup! This simple soup is so delicious, and I can feel my cells sucking up the nutrients when I drink this healing concoction. If ever I am not feeling my best, or if I have indulged in less than healthy foods (my clean and sensitive body always protests), I will make a pot of Green Immunity Soup and drink it for a day, or half a day, or just a couple of cups.
The point is to get these nutrients into the body so the cells, organs, tissues, etc…can Heal and Thrive!
This soup will be a little different every time, depending on what kinds of green vegetables you have on hand.
This is my favorite version!

---

1 pound broccoli, with stems cut into 1 inch chunks
1/2 a head cabbage, coarsely chopped
2 zucchinis, cut into 1 inch chunks
1 onion, chopped
2-3 cloves garlic, coarsely chopped
3 celery stalks, chopped into 1inch chunks
4 big kale leaves, ribs removed and coarsely chopped
Vegetable broth just to barely cover

Wash and cut up all the vegetables. Put everything into a big stock pot and bring to a boil. Reduce heat to medium low, cover and simmer for about 30 minutes, or until the vegetables are soft but not falling apart. Remove from heat, take off the lid and allow to cool completely at room temperature. When the soup is completely cool run the vegetables and broth through a blender until very smooth. You will need to do this in batches, so pour each batch into a second pot and stir the whole pot well after all the soup is blended and before pouring into individual jars or containers.

Store in the refrigerator for 4-5 days or freeze for up to 3 months.

You can easily half this recipe.

To your excellent health!

Creamy Cauliflower Soup

Serves 6

This is a very soul soothing soup on a cold evening!

Olive oil or canola spray
1 medium yellow onion, diced
5 cloves garlic, chopped
1 heaping tsp turmeric
1 medium head of cauliflower

3 cups vegetable broth
2-3 sprigs of fresh thyme, whole or
1 tsp dried thyme
1 - 13 ounce can coconut milk
Salt and pepper

Wash the cauliflower, remove and toss the leaves. Cut the florets away from the stalk Coarsely chop the florets and most of the stalk.

Spray a large stock pot and heat over medium high. Add the onions and sauté for 3-4 minutes. Add the chopped garlic, turmeric and cook for 1 minute. Add in the chopped cauliflower and stalk, vegetable broth and thyme. Stir well to combine and bring to a low boil. Reduce heat to medium low, cover and simmer for 30 minutes, until the cauliflower is very tender.

Remove the thyme sprigs and add the coconut milk. Stir well. Allow to cool.

In batches, puree the soup in a blender or use a hand blender, until very smooth, adding more vegetable broth if it is too thick.

Garnish with fresh chopped thyme and pepper.

Vegetable Broth

I compost…therefore I am…helping the environment!
When we eat Plant Based, we create a LOT of vegetable scraps.
So, why not use them to make one of the most common ingredients in this book?
You can save veggie scraps, peelings, trimmings, stems and cores for about
3 days in the refrigerator before you need to use them, or you can freeze them.
Just keep them in a sealed container until you are ready to make broth.

Simply put all of your vegetable scraps into a big stock pot, cover with water by about 2 inches and bring to a boil over high heat. Reduce the heat to medium-low and simmer for 30 minutes. You can add herbs, bay leaves, coriander, cumin and/or fennel seeds, black peppercorns if you like. It is best not to add salt to Homemade Broth. You may find that you don't need to add salt to dishes when you use this broth because it is so full of flavor.

Allow the Vegetable Broth to cool to room temperature, as the flavors continue to release and mingle. Strain through a fine-mesh strainer and compost the used vegetable scraps.

Most vegetable scraps are great for making broth. I would omit onion skins, artichoke scraps and eggplant peelings because they can make your broth taste bitter, and if you use garlic skins, just add one or two because your broth can become Uber Garlic Fragrant!

Allow the broth to cool completely before storing in glass jars. This Vegetable Broth will keep for about 10 days in the refrigerator, and 6 months in the freezer.

*If you are freezing Vegetable Broth (or any liquids like soup), fill the jar leaving at least 2 inches or more space at the top, cool completely to room temperature then allow to chill in the refrigerator for 1- 2 hours before moving to the freezer.

Sweets for the Sweet

Eat Your Vegetables, Bitches

Sweets for the Sweet

Ultra ~ Orange Cake

This recipe comes from the Buttercup Preschool class at Three Cedars Waldorf School in Bellevue, Washington, where my kiddos went to school for years.
I am not sure where the recipe originated, but it is a crowd pleaser!
My daughter, Chrissie is allergic to dairy, and this has been one of her favorites for years!
I like to make it in a Bundt pan because Bundt Cakes are pretty…and Bundt is fun to say!
It is a perfect cake for tea. It is not too sweet, and there is no sticky icing.

Preheat the oven to 350 degrees. Spray a Bundt pan with olive oil or canola spray.

*WHISK TOGETHER:
3 cups all-purpose flour
2/3 cup sugar
2 tsp baking soda
1 tsp salt

*IN A SEPARATE BOWL STIR TOGETHER:
1 1/2 cups orange juice
2/3 cup vegetable oil (walnut, avocado, canola)
1 TBLS grated orange zest
2 TBLS apple cider vinegar
2 tsp vanilla

*ADD THE WET INGREDITENTS TO THE DRY AND MIX UNTIL SMOOTH.

Scrape the batter into the pan and spread evenly. Bake until a toothpick inserted into the center comes out clean, about 30-35 minutes.

Allow to cool in the pan for about 5 minutes, then put a plate on top of the Bundt pan and invert. Allow to cool completely then sprinkle with a bit of powdered sugar and scatter raspberries around the cake.

Gluten Free Granola

Makes about 4 cups

1/2 cup gluten free oats
1/2 cup flax meal
1/4 cup (heaping) raw pumpkin seeds
1 cup raw chopped cashews, divided
1 TBLS vanilla
1/4 cup real maple syrup

1/4 cup olive oil
1 cup whole almonds, I like to use roasted and lightly salted
1/2 cup slivered almonds
1/2 cup chopped walnuts
1/4 cup dried fruit of your choice -
      cranberries, raisins, cherries.

Preheat the oven to 325 degrees.

Combine the oats, flax meal, pumpkin seeds and 1/2 cup of the cashews in a large bowl. Combine the vanilla, maple syrup and olive oil together, whisking well and drizzle over the oats and nuts. Toss to coat everything well. Spray a cookie sheet well with olive oil or canola spray. Spread the mixture onto the cookie sheet into an even layer approximately 1/2 inch of thickness. Bake for 18 minutes or until it is nearly dry and crispy. DO NOT OVERCOOK! KEEP AN EYE ON IT!

Allow the mixture to cool completely in the pan for about 45 minutes. After about 20 minutes loosen the mixture from the pan with a spatula and allow to continue cooling.

While the mixture is baking, combine the two types of almonds, the walnuts, the rest of the cashews and the dried fruit in the same bowl you used before.

Crumble the cooled mixture into the bowl of nuts and dried fruit. Stir well and store in the freezer. Serve with a scoop of vegan yogurt and/or fresh fruit.

Aunt Donna's Pie Crust

My BFF, Kim Bogan Goldman and I met in high school in Ms. Belisle's art class.
We could not have been more different from each other. She was a Senior and I was a Sophomore.
She was super outgoing and I very insecure and introverted. And yet, we clicked.
Forty-one years later we are still the very best of friends. Over the years we have found many
Karmic experiences that brought us together and have bound us as friends…sisters!
One of these many bonds is a passion for cooking, and dare I say eating!
This recipe for my favorite pie crust comes from Kim's husband, Bruce's Auntie Donna.
I have altered the ingredient amounts to allow for extra crust to "Build Up" edges!

---

2 1/2 cups sifted all-purpose flour
1 1/8 tsp salt

3/4 cups Earth Balance = 13 TBLS
1/2 cup COLD water

Sift the flour and salt into a bowl. Remove 1/2 cup of the flour/salt mixture and add to it the 1/2 cup cold water and mix until it forms a paste. Cut the Earth Balance into the remaining flour, then add the paste. Mix ONLY until it comes together. Start mixing with a spoon and pull it together with your hands. Separate into two balls of dough, wrap them in plastic wrap and refrigerate for 30 minutes before rolling out between two sheets of waxed paper. That's it! Enjoy!

All American Apple Pie

Makes 1 Pie

I like to use Granny Smith apples because they are tart, and the pie is not overly sweet.
The Tapioca thickens the juices, and soaking the Tapioca first leaves your pie smooth and without gelatinous Tapioca beads. You're welcome, Chrissie!

---

1 recipe Aunt Donna's Pie Crust - makes two crusts
+ extra to "build up" the edges.
2 TBLS minute Tapioca, soaked in 4 TBLS warm water
6 medium Granny Smith Apples,
peeled, cored and sliced

1/4 cup granulated sugar
1 tsp grated lemon zest
1 1/2 tsp cinnamon
1/2 tsp allspice
1 1/2 TBLS Earth Balance, in 6 or 8 small cubes

Preheat the oven to 350 degrees.

Measure the tapioca into a small bowl, cover with warm water and stir. Peel, core and slice the apples and put them into a large bowl. Stir together the sugar, lemon zest, cinnamon, allspice and soaked tapioca. Sprinkle over the apples and combine well. Allow to rest while you roll out the pie crusts.

Spray the pie pan and put one crust in the bottom, gently pressing down to fit the pie pan. Cut the edges off around the outside of the pie pan and save the dough. Pour the apple mixture into the bottom pie crust and place the cubes of Earth Balance on top of the apples, evenly spaced out. Place the second pie crust on top and crimp the edges. Or, cut strips of dough and lay them crisscross on top of the apples, weaving in and out. Take the leftover dough and roll it out. Using a pizza cutter, cut curved lines of dough 1 inch wide and place them around the edge of the pie, to "build up" the edges. Crimp the dough with your fingers. Make 4 slits in the top of the pie crust, just out from the center.

Bake in the preheated 350 degree oven for about 1 hour and 15 minutes, until the apples are bubbly, and the crust is golden brown. Allow to cool for 20 minutes before serving.

Eat Your Vegetables, Bitches

Pumpkin Pie

Makes 1 pie

This is Chrissie's favorite. She makes this for Thanksgiving and Christmas every year!

---

1 crust -Aunt Donna's Pie Crust, pre-baked at 400 degrees for 15 minutes *(Sweets for the Sweet)*
2 TBLS egg replacer mixed with 4-5 TBLS water or 2 Flax Eggs *(Sauces and Such)*
1/3 cup sugar
1 TBLS molasses
Pinch of salt
2 tsp cinnamon
1/2 tsp ground cloves
1/2 tsp allspice
3 TBLS cornstarch
1 – 15 oz can pumpkin puree (Not Pumpkin Pie Mix)
1 1/2 cups of coconut milk

Preheat oven to 400 degrees

First things first…roll out one pie crust and press it into a sprayed pie pan. Place parchment paper over the pie crust then put some raw beans on the parchment, spread evenly for weight. Gently press down. Bake in a 400 degree oven for 15 minutes. Remove the parchment and beans, and your crust is ready to fill.

Raise the heat to 450 degrees.

Combine the egg replacer and water and beat wildly until frothy.

Add in the sugar, molasses, salt, spices and cornstarch until well blended.

Add the pumpkin puree, coconut milk and mix well.

Pour into the prebaked pie crust and bake on the lower shelf of the oven for 10 minutes. Lower the heat to 400 degrees and bake for about 30 minutes. Remove from the oven and allow to cool. The filling will be soft but will firm up as it cools. Refrigerate before serving.

Mixed Berry Crisp

Serves 6

A crisp is so easy to make, and you can mix and match the fruit that goes in.
Feel free to use just blueberries or raspberries, or peaches…you get the idea!
This crisp comes together quite quickly, and served with almond or soy vanilla ice cream,
you will have a table full of plate lickers!

---

1 cup oats
1 cup walnuts
3/4 cup all-purpose or almond flour
4 TBLS Earth Balance
2 tsp cinnamon

1/4 tsp allspice
1/4 tsp cloves
1/4 cup sugar
6 cups mixed berries

Preheat oven to 375 degrees.

Put the oats, walnuts, flour, Earth Balance, cinnamon, allspice, cloves and sugar into the food processor. Pulse until everything is combined and the walnuts are coarsely chopped. DO NOT OVER PROCESS. Or it won't be crispy and crumbly!

Spray a 9 x 13 inch baking dish and add the mixed berries. (It is okay if the berries are frozen.)

Crumble the crisp mixture over the berries and spread out evenly.

Bake at 375 degrees for 30 minutes or until golden brown and bubbly.

Peach & Blueberry Cobbler

Serves 6

There is nothing more delicious in the summer than fresh peaches and blueberries! Yes, they are absolute perfection just as they are. But, sometimes I just gotta have some Cobbler! (Insert Southern accent here.) Oh Lord, I sound like my Mama! Yes, there is a lot of Butter-Like Substance in this recipe, but I am putting this out there as a special treat! Remember 90%-10%! This recipe lands smack in the 10% category!

---

4 cups fresh peaches, peeled and sliced
1 cup fresh blueberries
1 stick Vegan Earth Balance
1/4 cup plus 1 TBLS sugar

1 1/2 cups flour
2 TBLS baking powder
1 tsp vanilla
1 1/2 cups almond milk

Preheat oven to 375 degrees.

Peel and slice the peaches and set aside with the blueberries. In the oven, melt the Earth Balance in a 9 x 13 inch baking pan, about 3-5 minutes. While the Earth Balance is melting, combine the 1/4 cup of sugar, flour, baking powder, vanilla and almond milk in a bowl. Mix well. While hot from the oven, carefully pour the batter over the melted Earth Balance and place the sliced peaches and blueberries on top of the batter. Sprinkle with 1 TBLS of sugar. Bake at 375 degrees for 45 minutes.

*You can make this with just peaches or just blueberries or just about any fruit you like!

Raspberry Scones

Makes 10 Scones

2 cups all-purpose flour, plus a bit for rolling out
1/4 cup plus 1 TBLS sugar
1 TBLS baking powder
 Zest from 1 medium lemon
1/2 tsp salt
8 TBLS = 1 stick Earth Balance, cut into
        1/2 inch cubes and chilled

3/4 cup plus 1 TBLS plant based cream
        (I use TJ's Soy Creamer,
        and it works great!)
1 cup frozen raspberries, keep them frozen
        until they are called for

Preheat the oven to 400 degrees.

Combine the 2 cups of flour, 1/4 cup of sugar, baking powder, lemon zest and salt in a large bowl and whisk together, breaking up any lumps. Cut the Earth Balance into the flour mixture with a pastry blender until small, pea-sized pieces remain.

Lightly flour your work surface and rolling pin. Pour in the 3/4 cup of plant based cream, using your fingers to mix just until it starts to come together. It will not all be incorporated and it will be a sticky mound.   Turn the dough out onto your lightly floured work surface and gently knead just until the dough holds together. Form the dough into a rough rectangle, with the long edge toward you. Roll the dough into an 8 x 10 inch rectangle, keeping the long edge toward you.

Take the raspberries from the freezer and evenly arrange them in a single layer over the lower two-thirds of the rectangle, and press them into the dough. Some of them may break. It's okay!

Holding on to the top one-third of the rectangle (the part without berries), fold the dough over one third, then over one third again. *Use a spatula or scraper if the dough sticks to your work surface.

Flour the rolling pin again and gently roll the dough into a 1-inch-thick block. Square the ends with your fingers. Slice the block of dough into 5 squares, cutting straight down, do not saw back and forth. Cut each square diagonally into two triangles.

Transfer the scones to a lightly floured plate and pop them in the freezer for 5 minutes.

Remove the scones from the freezer and transfer to a sprayed cookie sheet, about 2 inches apart. Brush a thin layer of plant based cream on each scone and sprinkle with a bit of sugar. Bake until golden brown, about 20 minutes. Let them cool on the cookie sheet for 5 minutes, then transfer to a wire rack to cool.

Serve with tea!

Eat Your Vegetables, Bitches

Red Wine Poached Pears

Serves 6

This desert is so sophisticated, elegant and delicious, your guests will be in awe of your
"Mad Skills"! They do not need to know how simple it was to create.
Serve with a scoop of vanilla almond or soy ice cream and a mint leaf!
C'est magnifique!
Okay, some logistics. My favorite pears to poach are Bosc, Anjou and Asian, in that order.
Avoid Bartlett Pears because they are too soft.
As for the red wine, Cabernet Sauvignon or Merlot are both excellent choices.
And, buy an inexpensive bottle for poaching. Think two buck Chuck!
Make sure the saucepan you use is big enough for the pears to fit snugly.
You do not want them swimming around. They will start poaching standing up on their bottoms,
then will finish having their tops submerged, so choose a pan where you can tip the pears over and
submerge after the bottoms have poached.

---

1 – 4 inch x 2 inch piece of orange peel	3 cups red wine
10 whole cloves	1/2 cup water
1 cinnamon stick	2 tsp vanilla
2 star anise	6 medium sized pears, peeled just
1/3 cup sugar	before poaching…not before!

Put all the ingredients (except the pears) into a saucepan that allows the pears to stand up and not wiggle around too much. Bring the red wine mixture to a good simmer over medium high heat, stirring as the sugar dissolves. Turn heat to low and now peel the pears, leaving the stems and cut the bottoms off so they will sit flat. Gently put the pears into the red wine mixture, on their bottoms. Bring the heat up to medium-low and allow to poach standing for 10 minutes. Tip each pear onto its side, tops toward the middle and submerged. Allow to poach for another 10-12 minutes, turning every 3 minutes so the pears are poached on all sides.

Remove from heat and allow the pears to remain in the red wine to cool.

The pears can be served at room temperature or can be chilled after they cool.

Just before serving, move the poached pears to a plate and cover with plastic wrap.

Turn the heat to medium high under the red wine mixture and allow to simmer for about 10 minutes so the liquid becomes a syrup. Keep stirring and do not let it get too thick.

Serve on individual plates, drizzled with the syrup and a scoop of vegan vanilla ice cream. Garnish with a mint leaf.

Mango Sticky Rice

4 - 1/2 cup servings

In Thailand it's called khao niaow ma muang, and it is very scrumptious!
Thai restaurants seem to have Mango Sticky Rice only in the summertime.
But, in the USA mangos are usually always available. There are a variety of different Mangos,
each being in season at different times of the year, so you can usually find one.
This is a classic Thai desert and a simple recipe.
I add vanilla to my recipe to give it a little something extra! You can easily double this recipe.

---

1 cup sticky rice, rinsed well
1 1/2 cups of water
4 TBLS brown sugar
Pinch of salt
1 14oz can full fat coconut milk, shake well
1 tsp vanilla
1 or 2 ripe mangos
Fresh mint

Put the rinsed rice in a pot with 1 cup of the water and allow to soak for 20 minutes. Do not drain the rice. Add the other 1/2 cup of water and 1/2 of the can of coconut milk (stir the coconut milk with a whisk before adding), a pinch of salt and 1 TBLS of brown sugar. Stir well.

Over medium high heat, bring to a slow boil. Cover the pot leaving the lid off a bit to allow steam to rise. Reduce the heat to medium low and simmer gently for about 20-25 minutes, until all the liquid had been absorbed. Turn off the heat and allow the pot to sit for about 10 minutes.

Meanwhile, make the sauce by combining the remaining coconut milk, 3 TBLS of brown sugar and vanilla in a saucepan. Warm over medium-low heat until the sugar dissolves.

Cut the mango into 1 inch chunks.

Divide the rice into four bowls and drizzle the sweet coconut milk all over. Top with mango chunks and a mint leaf.

Enjoy!

Mini Churro Bites

Makes about 20

Foods can carry such powerful memories. For instance, the first time I had a churro was with my then boyfriend, Ronnie Provenzano, walking on the Santa Monica Pier. It was the sweetest, most delicious thing I had ever tasted. Or perhaps it was the company…probably both. I cannot see or smell churros without associating that sweet day with Ronnie. Thanks for the memories!

Chorro Bites
1 cup all-purpose flour
1/4 cup sugar
1 TBLS ground flax meal
1 tsp cinnamon
1 tsp baking soda
1/4 tsp salt
3/4 cup almond milk, unflavored and unsweetened
1/4 cup canola oil
1 tsp apple cider vinegar

Coating
1 TBLS sugar
1 1/2 tsp cinnamon

Preheat the oven to 350 degrees. Spray a mini muffin pan. You will need 24 or use 2 - 12 mini muffin pans.

Whisk together the flour, sugar, flax, cinnamon, baking soda and salt. Measure the almond milk, canola oil and apple cider vinegar together and stir. Whisk into the dry ingredients.

Spoon the batter into the muffin pans, filling them almost to the top.

Bake for 13-15 minutes. The top should spring back when pressed. Allow to cool in the pan for 5 minutes.

Combine the 1 TBLS of sugar and 1 1/2 tsp cinnamon in a small bowl. Roll the muffin bites in the cinnamon/sugar mix.

Serve with coffee or tea.

Banana Ice Cream

Makes about 4 servings

The #1 reason to freeze bananas!

---

5 ripe bananas, frozen
1-2 cups of Almond, Soy, Oat, Hemp or Coconut milk
2 tsp vanilla
Sprinkle of cinnamon

The bananas should be ripe, with some brown spots and easy to peel. Peel and cut the bananas into 2 inch chunks, place into a Ziplock bag and put into the freezer for about 8 hours.

When frozen, toss the bananas, vanilla and almond milk into the blender or food processor and blend until smooth.

*Start with 1 cup of milk and add more until creamy.

Sprinkle with cinnamon, and chopped nuts of your choice, if you like!

This is best if eaten the day you make it!

Themed Menu Plans

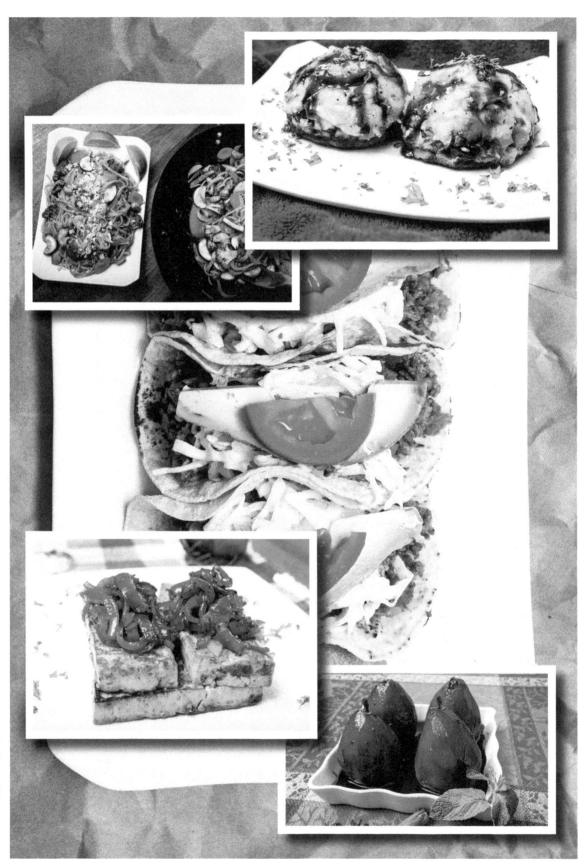

Eat Your Vegetables, Bitches

Themed Menu Plans

There are so many opportunities throughout the year to celebrate.
Gathering at the table is a time honored tradition that brings people together in community,
to break bread, share stories and celebrate life.
I hope you find many opportunities to sit down with the people you love!

~ Sunday Brunch ~

Fruit Salad with Fresh Herbs
Salads and Whatnot   195

Veggie Tofu Scramble
Breakfast of Champions   33

Rise & Shine Potatoes
Breakfast of Champions   34

Raspberry Scones
Breakfast of Champions   41

~ Spring Fling ~

Arugula, Spinach, Fennel & Strawberry Salad
Salads and Whatnot   181

Grilled Tofu with Red Onion Marmalade
Main Courses   118

Garlic and Chive Mashed Parsnips with Potatoes
On the Side   139

Roasted Asparagus
Green Things, Yellow Things, Red Things, Orange Things - See Roasted Broccoli   70

All American Apple Pie
Sweets for the Sweet   234

~ Summer Nights ~

Sweet Caramelized Figs with Vegan "Goat Cheese"
Hors d'Oeuvres   48

My Classic Dinner Salad
Salads and Whatnot   176

Ratatouille over Vegan Cheesy Polenta
Green Things, Yellow Things, Red Things, Orange Things   62   -   On the Side   135

Peach and Blueberry Cobbler
Sweets for the Sweet   239

~ Autumn Harvest ~

The BEST Butternut Squash Soup
Soups and Stews   *213*

Cabbage Rolls
Main Courses   *85*

Roasted Fingerling Potatoes & Brussels Sprouts
On the Side   *136*

Pumpkin Pie
Sweets for the Sweet   *237*

~ Winter Chill ~

Italian Kale Salad

Magical Mulligatawny

Rootin' Tootin' Crootins'

Mixed Berry Crisp

~ When In Greece... ~

Greek Salad in the Round
Salads and Whatnot   179

Dolmades with Tzatziki
Main Courses   116   -   Sauces and Such   159

Baked Greek Veggies
Green Things, Yellow Things, Red Things, Orange Things   73

Rice Pilaf
On the Side   142

Ultra ~ Orange Cake
Sweets for the Sweet   232

~ A Thai Feast ~

Crispy Baked Tofu with Finger Lickin' Peanut Sauce
Hors d'Oeuvres   57

Finger Lickin' Peanut Sauce
Sauces and Such...   172

Veggie Pad Thai
Main Courses   109

Thai Basil Eggplant
Main Courses   128

Mango Sticky Rice
Sweets for the Sweet   244

~ Italiano ~

Antipasto Salad
Salads and Whatnot   189

Eggplant Lasagna
Main Courses   83

Roasted Broccoli
Green Things, Yellow Things, Red Things, Orange Things   70

Banana Ice Cream with chopped pistachios
Sweets for the Sweet   246

~ Mexican Fiesta ~

Awesome Guacamole
Hors d'Oeuvres   50

Fresh Mexican Salsa, Olé
Sauces and Such...   168

CauliWally Tacos
Main Courses   95

Pot 'O Pinto Beans
Beans, Beans   150

Spanish Rice
On the Side   144

Mini Churro Bites
Sweets for the Sweet   245

~ Holiday Dinner ~

Un-Traditional Caesar Salad
Salads and Whatnot   184

Shepherd's Pie Portobellos
Main Courses   124

Spiralized Sweet Potatoes with Garlic and Herbs
Green Things, Yellow Things, Red Things, Orange Things   68

Brussels Sprouts Extraordinaire
Green Things, Yellow Things, Red Things, Orange Things   63

Spiced Cranberry Sauce
Sauces and Such...   167

Red Wine Poached Pears with vegan Vanilla Ice Cream
Sweets for the Sweet   243

Index

D

E

F

G

Q

R

S

T

CPSIA information can be obtained
at www.ICGtesting.com
Printed in the USA
JSHW052110140521
14733JS00005B/1